KENTUCKY'S HAUNTED GRAVEYARDS

The Frightening Floyds

Nightmare Press
Shepherdsville, KY

JACOB FLOYD AND JENNY FLOYD

KENTUCKY'S HAUNTED GRAVEYARDS

Dedicated to our beloved Bombay cat, Bat-Bat, originally named Spooky Maleficent Toombs, then became Baby Bat, and is now Bat-Bat. She's the best!!!

JACOB FLOYD AND JENNY FLOYD

Other works by The Frightening Floyds
Haunts of Hollywood Stars and Starlets
Aliens Over Kentucky
Strange and Unusual Mysteries
Be Our Ghost
Kentucky's Strange and Unusual Haunts
Jenny's Spooky Little Tales: Vol. 1
Jenny's Spooky Little Tales: Vol. 2

KENTUCKY'S HAUNTED GRAVEYARDS

The Frightening Floyds

JACOB FLOYD AND JENNY FLOYD

INTRODUCTION

KENTUCKY'S HAUNTED GRAVEYARDS

This book contains some previously released material—some of which we have added new information to (especially the Lexington Cemetery), and some that was in books currently out of print (but will return one day soon!). We know some folks may not want to read a book of haunts as large as *Kentucky's Strange and Unusual Haunts* to find all the graveyards. Not to mention, some, like Cave Hill and Eastern Cemetery, we didn't include in that book, as those were chapters in *Louisville's Strange and Unusual Haunts*, so we decided to make a small book dedicated only to the cemeteries.

On top of rewritten and revised tales from previous books, we have a few that are new as well—such as Hebron Cemetery and the mausoleum at Evergreen. There are also some locations that aren't haunted, but haunting, and a couple that are simply interesting tidbits of knowledge. Sometimes, when you're a paranormal researcher, new information comes to light and you have to amend past works. Considering we had a fair amount of new and updated information, we figured a separate book for graveyards was in order.

So, if cemeteries are your thing, have a seat and enjoy our little tome—*Kentucky's Haunted Graveyards*.

Jacob and Jenny Floyd

TABLE OF CONTENTS

LOUISVILLE'S NECROPOLIS

Louisville's Strange and Unusual Haunts

JACOB FLOYD AND JENNY FLOYD

One cannot talk about Louisville cemeteries without mentioning Cave Hill. As far as lands for resting places go, it is the city's premier haven for the dead. Not only is it a massive field of rolling hills, reaching trees, and magnificent artistic monuments, it is also a tourist attraction known for having interred a few prominent people and celebrities. Among them are Col. Harland Sanders, George Rogers Clark, the former Frito Lay magician Harry Collins, and the legendary boxing icon, Muhammad Ali.

A plethora of former politicians, landowners, and past powerhouse millionaires whose names appear all over Louisville street signs, hospitals, parks, and other various forms of public architecture lay in peace beneath these grounds. It also hosts the American Union Monument of Louisville for unknown soldiers of the Civil War, as well as the 32nd Indiana Monument, which honors the Union soldiers of the 32nd Indiana Volunteer Infantry Regiment that gave their lives near Munfordville, Kentucky on December 17th, 1861 in the Battle of Rowlett's Station. Both of which, along with Cave Hill itself, have been placed on the National Historic Registry.

This breathtaking Victorian cemetery and arboretum ties together the intersection at Baxter Avenue and Bardstown Road in the Highlands neighborhood, an area known for bars, restaurants, and local shops. Surrounded by a massive brick wall topped with no-nonsense razor wire, this nearly three-hundred-acre burial ground started as farm east of Louisville before being chartered in 1848. Now, with all the winding paths, opulent structures, hilltop gravesites, and various ponds and fountains, Cave Hill is more than just a graveyard, it's a veritable city of the dead.

And, it's not without its share of haunts.

Now, some investigators deride us for our affinity of graveyards and cemeteries in regards to our methods of investigations. But, we believe that many spirits would probably remain near their graves, watching over their former vessels. Even if that weren't the case, historically speaking, no one knows every event that has occurred on these grounds that may anchor a spirit in place. Jenny's nickname is "Graveyard Girl" to some, and though meant as a snide remark, she embraces it with pride. Some of the strangest occurrences we've had ourselves have been in graveyards and cemeteries, and one of our first was right here in Cave Hill.

Now, when we investigate, Jenny and I are not a big production, and our equipment isn't as sophisticated and high-tech as the well-funded groups most often seen searching for spectral evidence via graphs and gauges. We will not tell you we are scientists though we firmly believe science can explain many phenomena, but also staunchly believe that answers can come from psychological, metaphysical, and parapsychological means, as well. Skepticism is healthy, but it must be open-minded since none of us really knows anything about the beyond and what rests there.

But, no matter where the explanations come from, the ultimate reality is that you will never convince a hardcore skeptic, and if you do, it's going to require irrefutable visual evidence, which can only come in the form of video or photography. All the readings of lights, temperatures, and voices mean nothing to a skeptic. So, when we "ghost hunt," we simply bring two digital cameras, a video camera, a laptop as a stationary camera, a digital recorder, dowsing rods, a meter or two, and a spirit box—and that's when we are seriously planting ourselves in place for the evening. But, when we go into cemeteries, we bring only our cameras, spirit box, and maybe digital recorder and meter.

We had heard tales of green lights and orbs floating about Cave Hill at night, as well as strange noises and voices in the darkness. Reports of tombstones suddenly falling over, as if having been pushed, exist as well. The grounds are gated shut after five in the afternoon, but our opinion is that a ghost is a ghost and they'll be there day or night. An investigation does not require the shade of nighttime in order for one to catch a glimpse into the afterlife. We have captured quite a bit during the day. To us, waiting for nightfall is a dramatic effect, beyond the belief of the Devil's Hours, which occur in the middle of the night. While it might be easier to catch shadows, orbs, mists, and apparitions in the contrast that occurs between flashbulb and darkness, a manifestation can just as easily appear under the t glare of the sun. So, we packed up our stuff and went into Cave Hill in broad daylight several times to see what we could find.

One of Louisville's soft spring drizzles marred our first drive. But, when we fired up the spirit box, passing backwards quickly through radio channels, we started to hear some clear statements made in the dead air between frequencies—statements much too long to be radio. Some of them were hard to make out, but we did hear, *Hear comes the rain*, mixed in. At one point, when I was trying to back up and drive back to a turn I had missed, we both heard, *Watch out!* ring out from the box. I hit the brakes and looked behind me, then saw that our bumper was mere inches away from someone's tombstone. Glad somebody was watching!

During the visit, we also came to a row of Charnel Houses dug into the side of one of the many small hills bubbling across the land. We snapped several photos of this area and didn't know until we reviewed the pictures that there was one that seemed to have a shape of a slender man's profile, arms out, with his mouth open, drawn across the facade. This took shape in the lichen, mold, and moss that had sprouted on the stone over the years.

Now, many people would chalk this up to a psychological term used around the paranormal community a lot: pareidolia—a belief that people make shapes and patterns out of nothing—something we believe, no doubt, happens quite often. But, as we always try to remain both objective and open to all matters of explaining the mysterious, we also think that it is possible for spiritual energies to show themselves through the natural sources of the world, such as rain mists, sunlight, shadows, and even molds, and this could be a possible example of such an occurrence.

Over time, this shape has barely altered, though the "facial" area seems to be slowly fading. Maybe it is just coincidental shape forming, or maybe it is the man buried within claiming his territory.

Up towards the top of the cemetery's highest hill, near the war monuments, is a small, circular path beneath some overhanging trees that hover above some graves. This spot has been noisy a few times for us. Our first trip up there ended quickly after some angry voices spoke from the spirit box, followed by footsteps, and the tossing of a couple of rocks at our car. Other times we have gone there, we have heard the voices on the box again, and the crunching of nearby fallen branches, but never anymore flying rocks.

We captured one of our earliest pictures on that aforementioned rainy day. Often times, we just randomly snap pictures of the areas we investigate, and many times Jenny will discover something strange in the background. There are a few occasions where I have, too, but mostly they come from her thorough research. On this day, I was performing my unorganized picture-taking display all around Cave Hill and, when Jenny later reviewed the pictures, she found something unusual far away in the background. It took the zoom option to its limit, but far away, against a tree, seemingly sitting on a stone—or possibly leaning against the tree—is the transparent apparition of a man who looks to have dark hair, looking towards the sky. Jokingly, we named him Charlie Chaplin for his appearance. The picture is grainy and blurry, but once you see him, you notice him every time.

While most haunts there are harmless, there may be a sinister spirit, and he hangs out by the grave of the Frito Lay Magician, Harry Collins. We do not believe it is the magician himself.

Our first time visiting his monument and grave, Jenny and a friend of hers stood before the life-sized statue of Mr. Collins with the spirit box running. While there were some hard to tell responses and voices on the box, words such as "penny," "coins," "cards," and the names of the various suits in a playing card deck could be heard. Often times, visitors to the site will put cards in the statue's hands, or a penny in its ear, and even lay magic-related items at its feet. Perhaps, he was referring to the items all about him.

While reviewing a picture I took around the area, Jenny found a strange orange shape reflected on the backside of a nearby tombstone. Though very hard to define, it looked possibly like a red or orange-colored face. With nothing in that area to cast such a reflection, we both found it to be strange, especially when we applied it to something that happened on the spirit box not long before we left.

As they were beginning to wrap up the session, Jenny ended the sweep on the radio, and the station it landed on blared out a long, loud, deep rumble that did not stop until they turned the spirit box off.

Later on, the friend reported to us that while she was at home several days later, discussing the trip to the magician's grave, a family member became disturbed and had sought confirmation if she said it was a magician's grave they visited. When she told him it was, he became nervous and told her that a few nights before, while lying in bed, he felt the presence of something standing near him just before he heard someone whisper the word, "magic."

During another visit to the statue, with just the two of us, Jenny stood before the monument, staring into its eyes, holding the spirit box in her hand. She felt a presence upon her, and as she stepped up to stand right in front of the sculpture, she asked, "Where's your stuff?" This was in reference to the absence of all the cards, coins, and random items people had laid about the plot. From the spirit box, clear as day, came the response, "That's too close."

As if that wasn't chilling enough, later in the conversation, Jenny asked, "Do you want to talk to me?" The box then answered, "I already have." We recorded this session on video and uploaded it to our YouTube channel. It is quite a peculiar thing, and it definitely tests the skepticism that I keep in my mind.

Cave Hill is a gorgeous place, full of great sculptures, monuments, and greenery, but it also appears that some of the spirits of the dead population therein still like to wander about the place, occasionally making their presence known to the many visitors the place sees throughout the year. If you're a paranormal enthusiast, or just morbid like us and enjoy visiting cemeteries, or if you like to view structures erected to represent splendor, then we recommend you taking a nice little drive around this fine historical landmark. Just don't make a spectacle of yourself if you decide to try a little ghost hunting on the sly.

DW IS WATCHING

Haunts of Hollywood Stars and Starlets

JACOB FLOYD AND JENNY FLOYD

Located in Oldham County, in the small town of Centerfield, KY, just outside of Louisville suburb Crestwood, Mt. Tabor Methodist Church has been a place of worship for the area since 1835. Centerfield is an ordinary American small town. But, there is one interesting fact about the unincorporated community: It is the final resting place of a once-famous Hollywood pioneer – DW Griffith.

These days, the director's name has faded from notoriety, accept among film aficionados and Hollywood historians. But, David Wark Griffith was one of the most significant figures in the early days of Hollywood, and is considered one of the most innovative and creative filmmakers of his era. Alongside prolific actress Mary Pickford, "King of Hollywood" Douglas Fairbanks, and legendary icon Charlie Chaplin, Griffith founded the production company United Artists in 1919, though his association with the studio was brief. The company's growing success led to MGM buying it in 1981. Today, Amazon MGM Studios own it, which also owns Orion Pictures, American International Pictures, and many other smaller media businesses.

Griffith made more than 500 films during a career that spanned from 1908 to 1931. By today's standards, that's an impossible number for a filmmaker to hit. But in the Silent Film Era, film production moved much faster. Still, even by the standards of that era, it's still a very prolific catalog. Among his most notable films are *Broken Blossoms, Way Down East,* and *Orphans of the Storm.* But, none of his works are more remembered than the controversial *Birth of a Nation,* released in 1915, which has been criticized for downplaying slavery, portraying the Ku Klux Klan as heroes, and for promoting an overall racist view of black people in America. There were riots in the north over the film's content. Despite this, *Birth of a Nation* became Hollywood's first blockbuster, as it was very popular. In response to the backlash, Griffith followed up with *Intolerance*, in which he meant to portray the dangers of intolerant thought. The film didn't do well at the box office, but redeemed Griffith in the eyes of many critics.

Griffith's legacy reduced to the creation of a racist film, earning him the label of a racist. Some argue the filmmaker was making a film representing the message of the source material (*The Clansmen* by Thomas Dixon, Jr.), aligned with some prevailing views of the time, as opposed to a personal political or social statement. Although his father was a Confederate Colonel during the Civil War, there's no evidence to suggest Griffith had any opinion on racial politics. Of course, it's justified that time would remember such a film as *Birth of a Nation* in a negative light, but upon further investigation and objective consideration, that does not necessarily mean it reflects the personal views of the man who made the movie. After all, one of the most popular sayings among creatives is that creators are not necessarily the art they create. It is perfectly reasonable to believe that Griffith was simply making a movie based on an idea, and did all he could to capture that prevailing philosophy, and nothing more.

Or, he really could have been a raging bigot. Who knows? Despite all that, many iconic filmmakers have praised his work as a craftsman in the industry, Cecil B. DeMille, Stanley Kubrick, and Alfred Hitchcock among them. Russian filmmaker Sergei Eisenstein spoke of Griffith as an "outstanding master" of the art, but criticized *Birth of a Nation* as "disgraceful propaganda of racial hatred towards the colored people," a comment in itself that would be considered racist in today's social climate.

If you have read our book *Haunts of Hollywood Stars and Starlets*, you will have read about some of Griffith's alleged haunts. Allegedly, he haunts the tenth-floor steps of the Knickerbocker Hotel, where he lived during the last days of his life, and where he passed away. He also haunts the area around his plot in the Mt. Tabor Methodist Church Cemetery. People have reported seeing his transparent specter standing around his grave, watching the world; or walking around his family plot. Witnesses describe his apparition as wearing a wide-brimmed Stetson and fedoras, along with the fine coats he wore in life.

Since having published our collection of Hollywood icons and some of their ghost stories, we have visited Griffith's grave on a few occasions. While, we've never seen his ghost, or experienced any disembodied sounds or paranormal incidents, we have, each time, encountered difficulty filming or conducting a spirit box session there.

We have attempted spirit box sessions there a few times. The first time, the box did just fine. We didn't receive any responses the first few minutes. When Jacob turned on the camera, which had a fully charged battery, everything was fine. But, when he started talking about the controversy of *Birth of a Nation* and the negative remarks cast upon Griffith for that film, the device froze. So, Jacob tried again. At first, it worked, but once he brought up the controversy, it froze again. The third time he tried, it wouldn't even record. At that point, the spirit box shut off.

When we returned to the car, Jacob tried the camera again, just to make sure there wasn't any malfunction, and it worked perfectly, never freezing. Jenny turned on the spirit box to see if the batteries had died, and it worked just fine. So, we decided to go back to the grave. Once there, the camera wouldn't even turn on. The spirit box turned on, but made no sound, and would not scan. The red light indicated the power worked was on, but there was nothing but dead air coming from the speakers. We relented and left.

We went back again maybe a year or more later, with the same camera and spirit box. Both devices had worked fine on many other occasions. When we got to DW Griffith's grave, it was as though his spirit remembered us. The camera wouldn't stay on. As soon as Jacob turned it on, it shut off. The battery still had energy, because it would turn on when we got back to the car. It just wouldn't stay on. The spirit box whined, and then wouldn't filter through the channels. It was apparent Mr. Griffith had no interest in speaking to us.

We haven't gone back since. These were certainly peculiar incidents. Maybe they weren't paranormal, but they sure make for a good laugh, and a little bit of eyebrow raising.

JACOB FLOYD AND JENNY FLOYD

PET HAVEN

Pets have become like children to many people in our society. At the very least, they are part of the family. To those who do not have children, they very much *are* their children. Some even choose to have pets in lieu of children.

But what do we do after our beloved fur-babies have departed from this world? Some choose to bury them in their yards. Others may have them cremated. There is even a new service that will turn your pet into taxidermy. Well, for those who do not want to stuff their dead pets, nor burn their remains, or don't have a yard in which to bury them, Shepherdsville has another option – Pet Haven Cemetery, down Highway 44.

If you don't already know the location as you travel that narrow, twisting end of the highway, you're likely to miss Pet Haven, whether you're looking for it or not. You might notice the odd letters stuck in the ground out front, but be unable to read them as you're passing by. Even the different map apps don't always take you to the right spot. If you do manage to find it, and you pull in, you'll definitely find yourself in an interesting, and even saddening, graveyard.

Scattered about the front, there are many markers and monuments for pets long gone. Some even have pictures on them. These are legitimate stones, with names and dates etched upon them. Though we were unable to find out an exact date to mark the beginning of Pet Haven, the current owner believes the year of opening was 1956. We do recall seeing graves dated as far back as the sixties. Even if we don't know the exact date, Pet Haven has provided a resting place for the deceased darlings for more than sixty years.

While it's not like the scary little burial ground from the Stephen King novel, it does have a disturbing history, a very macabre story, and some spooky energy.

Back in 2017, Pet Haven almost closed. The owners at the time were not properly maintaining the grounds. There were many patches where the grass was too high to see any graves. A lot of debris from wind and storms lay scattered about, making navigation both difficult and dangerous. Reports of people digging up plots have surfaced. One patron even said they found the site where their beloved pet lay in rest covered with plywood and other items to keep the hole from being visible.

The final straw came when someone noticed the marker for the grave they purchased missing. When she asked Pet Haven on their Facebook page, the owners replied they were closing the cemetery down. This led to questions regarding what people should do with their pets, to which the answer was they might want to dig their pets up and find somewhere else to bury them. The owners gave the customers a month to remove the remains, and then stated they would be raising private property posts, closing the land to the public.

Naturally, there was a great outcry of concern, with many people seeking legal counsel. After some research, people found there were no Kentucky laws dealing with animal remains, only human. The concerned populace took advice to pursue civil action if this sell would cause any contractual violations.

During this fiasco, others reported finding the graves of their pets disturbed. Rumors of stacked graves began to surface. There were accusations that the owners at the time buried multiple animals together to save space. No confirmation of this claim exists. We can say we are skeptical about this claim because there remains plenty of land at Pet Haven to inter many more animals. So, it is doubtful, but still possible. Either way, Pet Haven was a wreck and looked abandoned.

Thankfully, this matter was settled when current owner Joni Blake stepped in and purchased Pet Haven. With the help of volunteers, she was able to clear the three-and-a-half acres of land with a lot of weed eating, cleaning, and care. Now, it once again looks like a respectable place, with regular maintenance. Blake has moved to get the land historically registered as protection from closure or use by other purposes. As people who are not only pet lovers, but also have a few pets there ourselves, we are very thankful for Joni Blake's revitalization efforts.

It is a good thing Blake took over Pet Haven. Not just because she saved and restored it back to respectability, but also because of a macabre discovery made on a road in Shepherdsville back in 2020. One that is quite harrowing.

A woman on Memorial Day weekend came out of her house to see a flock of carrion birds gathered around an object on the side of the road. Upon investigation, she discovered it was a dead miniature donkey wrapped in plastic and left to decay. She called various agencies around the county, and none would do anything about it. After calling one of her friends to tell them of her discovery, her friend took a closer look at the carcass and was shocked to find the authorities wouldn't do anything to help. That's when they decided to call Pet Haven.

Blake, along with a man named Allen Bagby, came to the site and found, to their horror, there was not just one, but two, slain miniature donkeys. But that isn't all. The scene became much more gruesome as Blake and Bagby discovered the killers mutilated both donkeys: their limbs all severed, and both decapitated. One wore a harness, indicating it was likely someone's pet. Whomever committed this heinous act chopped these poor animals up and threw them on the side of the road as if they never mattered. Such a vile act is beyond contemptable, and we can only hope the perpetrator, or perpetrators, suffer proper justice.

In a truly magnanimous move, one that any true animal lover would applaud, Blake and Bagby sadly gathered the remains, took them to Pet Haven, and gave them the burial they deserved. Even more than that, Blake specially ordered two donkey statues to mark their resting places, near the giant cat statue towards the back of the cemetery. Though their names were never known, Blake and Bagby named them Jenny and Jack.

We are sorry to report that no suspect for this depraved crime exists. Worse than that, no one has even bothered to cover it. Not even the news stations. So, we are glad at least these poor souls had the fine people at Pet Haven Cemetery to lay them properly to rest.

Now, we suppose the question you are asking is if Pet Haven Cemetery is haunted. Even though we dug around, we could not find anything overwhelmingly interesting on that front. We have been told the place is haunted, but never been given any solid leads. The most we know is someone saw a transparent ghost dog standing in an open area, and running across the back. We were also told of a black cat wandering the graveyard before disappearing (which could have easily been a stray cat "disappearing" into the wooded area surrounding three-fourths of the cemetery). Someone told us they've heard a cat meowing when no cat was visible, but again – the copse of trees around Pet Haven provides plenty of space for a cat to hide.

On a personal note: One day, Jenny decided to visit Pet Haven when Jacob was working on some projects. Towards the back, she became uneasy. She felt as though something was watching her. Jenny has a knack for picking up on spiritual energy, and has found many of the out-of-the-way, or off-the-beaten-path, haunted locations we have written about in the past, simply by picking up on something and having me go in to inquire about any possible paranormal activity experienced there. While she was towards the back of Pet Haven, she saw a figure at the very edge of the property, near the woods, and thought it was watching her. She quickly took a picture and sent it to Jacob.

Upon reviewing it, Jacob thought it looked like a statue of Jesus. So, he and Jenny returned to Pet Haven so he could investigate. As he drew closer to the back, he began to feel the same oppressive energy. While Jacob often has the ability to "read the room" or notice what others are feeling, he doesn't consider himself in tune with paranormal energy. Though he has had some incidents when he has felt something seemingly sad or dark lingering. That day, what he felt was not necessarily dark, but heavy, maybe sad, and a bit eerie.

As he stood staring at the back section, he looked to the edge of the property and saw the statue. He told Jenny he saw it, and he could tell it was a statue. Jenny did not want to get any closer, as she was no doubt feeling the sadness in the air even more than was Jacob. So, Jacob walked to the statue and saw, sure enough, that it was a statue of Jesus facing the woods.

JACOB FLOYD AND JENNY FLOYD

In that little corner, there were many religious icons and statues gathered around the monuments. The energy there felt even eerier. He took some pictures of the area before we left.

Among the most interesting statues he saw back there was the large cat marking a rather spacious gravesite. Near that cat were the two donkey statues. This was before Jenny had heard about the slain donkeys and told Jacob about it. After we heard the story, we decided that was the source of the oppressive feelings. With it having been such a sad event—committed by someone who no doubt carries dark energy—that would explain the feelings both of us felt there.

More than because of that, we wanted to include Pet Haven Cemetery in this book to draw attention to the location. If you're in the area, please visit. Show your support in helping Joni Blake protect the land by getting it historically registered. Also, if you ever hear anything that could help give an idea about who murdered those sweet miniature donkeys, please come forward. Maybe those monsters can face justice.

THE FINAL RESTING PLACE OF FLOYD COLLINS

Kentucky's Strange and Unusual Haunts

JACOB FLOYD AND JENNY FLOYD

Stretching more than four-hundred miles beneath the grounds of west south-central Kentucky, Mammoth Cave is the longest known cave system in the world. Historians believe humans have used the cave for more than five-thousand years. Explorers have found mummified Native American remains there as far back as the 19th century. The earliest documentation of travels and explorations of the cave system dates back to the late 1700s, by the Pollard Survey.

If you've read *Kentucky's Strange and Unusual Haunts*, you will have read the various accounts of alleged paranormal activity. We will not cover all those here. However, we will, talk about the man who died there, only to have his body remain in the system for some time – local cave explorer, Floyd Collins.

Floyd lived during the Kentucky Cave Wars, where the various private owners of different caves in the area were competing over the increasing tourist traffic of the time. Floyd owned a section called the Crystal Cave, which he discovered in 1917, and it was losing the war due to no lodging and difficulty reaching the entrance. So, on January 30th, 1925, he decided to begin excavating an entrance into the Sand Cave nearby to make his own cave more accessible and appealing to the affluent tourists. But, he broke one of the most fundamental rules of cave exploration: he went alone and didn't tell anyone where he was going. While navigating his way through a very tight squeeze, Floyd found himself pinned by a boulder and trapped in the cave.

Someone later discovered him stuck in the hole. A media frenzy then ensued as radio stations and newspapers were keeping listeners and readers updated on Floyd's condition.

The more morbid-minded people gathered at the cave to watch the drama unfold, setting up food stands and selling souvenirs in the process. Meanwhile, Floyd was slipping further away beneath the soil of Central Kentucky. Rescuers attempted to move the massive boulder from Floyd's leg, but could not. A cave-in then occurred, blocking him off from all help. Two weeks later, Floyd died of exposure.

Due to the difficulty rescuers had reaching his body, Floyd remained where he died as funeral services took place on the surface. His family was not pleased that his body remained stuck in the Sand Cave, so his brother Homer managed to reach the corpse two months later and pull him out. His family buried him in a grave at the family farm near Crystal Cave, now known as Floyd Collins's Crystal Cave.

In 1927, Floyd's father Lee sold the cave and property to a dentist named Thomas. Thomas managed to get permission to have Floyd's body exhumed and moved to the entrance of Sand Cave, where it lay in a glass-lidded coffin for all the tourists to see.

As if this isn't bizarre enough, someone stole Floyd's body in 1929 and left it in a field, missing a leg. Most people figured this to be the act of rival cave owners who were angered by the amount of tourist attention the corpse was getting. After the leg's recovery, the entire body placed back in the coffin, but without the viewing lid—though many tourists peeked anyway.

The National Cave Systems purchased the Sand Cave in 1961 and closed it to tourism. One would think that an organization such as this would not only remove the body of Floyd Collins and give it a proper burial, but would make it high on the priority list. However, for whatever reason, that did not transpire until 1989, leaving Floyd to decay in the Sand Cave for almost thirty more years. It took a team of fifteen men to remove the casket and the tombstone, and Floyd Collins went into a proper grave at Mammoth Cave Baptist Church Cemetery, at the request of his family.

If ever a spirit had a reason to be in a state of unrest and haunt an area and its people, it would be that of Floyd Collins. His death was unfortunate, and the events occurring after were outright ludicrous. So, it really comes as no surprise to learn that there have been numerous witnesses to ghostly goings-on near where Floyd lost his life.

In the past, people have reported hearing a man's voice calling for help when near the spot where Floyd died. It's been said the phrase, "Help me, Johnny, I'm trapped!" has been heard—or some variation of that. Others have even described the sounds as "wailing cries for help." When looking around after these occurrences, people have found no one near, though the sounds continued.

There have also been accounts of rocks thrown through the darkness, at an angle that suggests it had not fallen from above, but had come in from the side. Could this be Floyd showing his anger over his corpse's abuse?

If it is him, we don't know if he's very angry. Colleen O'Conner Olson had an experience while exploring in one of Floyd's old spots. She told Wave 3 news in Kentucky that she had started to fall and felt someone grab her and pull her back up. Naturally, she thought it was her caving partner. But, when she turned to thank him, she found that he was on the other side of the cave. She then said, "Thanks Floyd."

But, the cave system isn't the only part of the park that is supposed to be haunted. People have reported strange occurrences along the Heritage Trail. Misty apparitions and transparent shadow-like images supposedly move along and around the trail; disembodied voices from nearby have been heard when it was clear no one else was around. The most chilling incident reported from the Heritage Trail is a pair of legs with no upper-body walking down the path. This pair of legs allegedly walks towards and away from people in plain view at distances close enough for witnesses to tell they have no upper body. Undoubtedly, this is the most sensational of all the claims that we have uncovered at Mammoth Cave National Park. Nonetheless, if we are willing to believe a full body ghost can manifest, why not a spirit only capable of partial manifestation?

Mammoth Cave—as old as the Earth itself—there's no telling what all has happened there, or who has died, and by what means, in that lightless labyrinth beneath the hardened dirt of Cave City. With so much uncharted territory that most believe still snakes its way through the underground, there might be further historic evidence and frightening ghosts waiting down there for someone to discover. If it is indeed a passage between our world and theirs, maybe one day some brave explorers will dig deep enough and find some answers waiting in the beyond.

It's an interesting thought, at least.

JACOB FLOYD AND JENNY FLOYD

THE FORGOTTEN CEMETERY

Kentucky's Strange and Unusual Haunts

KENTUCKY'S HAUNTED GRAVEYARDS

Tucked away in the corner of First Street Park in the town of Shepherdsville, Ky. is an old graveyard that is no longer used. Many residents don't even know it's there, hidden behind the plastic white picket fence; this cemetery is called the Old Pioneer Graveyard. It is one of the main attractions on the *Jacob Floyd's Shepherdsville History and Haunts Tour*. It intrigued most of our guests as we guided them through the dark, with Jacob leading by lantern light; most of them liked to snap pictures in hopes of catching a glimpse of one of the alleged ghosts rumored to wander the grounds. A few guests have captured streaks of light, strange mists, and even a peculiar outline of a man somewhere in the nearby woods. We're not telling you these are ghosts, but there has been a history of strange occurrences reported within this graveyard.

We call it the "Forgotten Graveyard" because at one time it was most certainly that. Looking to be near, or even over, two-hundred years old, this small cemetery has endured a lot of hardship through the ages. Upon entering, you can immediately tell this tiny burial ground has suffered the wrath of time, as many stones are cracked and broken, worn and dirty. As you look about the grounds, you can see where stones used to be but are now gone. Towards the side entrance, there are hardly any tombstones at all. If you're not careful, you might step in one of the holes where a headstone used to be.

By all appearances, it seems as though this was once the only graveyard in the city. Rumors of a small settlement somewhere in the area surrounding this graveyard—dating back to the early days of Shepherdsville, or even before—have surfaced, though there is no evidence to support this. But, what we do know is that this graveyard has some of the city's most prominent past members interred.

Shepherdsville, located right next to the Salt River, has seen many floods over the last two centuries, including the Great Flood of 1937 that affected many riverside towns up and down the Ohio and other smaller rivers. The last big flood the town had seen was in 1997, which wiped out many homes (including Jenny's when she was a child) throughout the historic district. Over the decades, the old graveyard has seen a lot of flood damage. Many stones have disappeared as a result, and there have been rumors of coffins and even bodies washing up. But, the latter may be nothing more than urban legend as no documentation of these incidents exists to our knowledge. We think this rumor grew from a hole located towards the back of the graveyard that has a crumbled, brick structure inside it. There has been much speculation as to what this might be: but a sinkhole is one theory; some think it may have been a grave, and the structure once inside, or perhaps on top (as if a sepulcher), was destroyed; someone may have even tried to rebuild it, only to find it taken apart again. The sepulcher theory is interesting because there is a busted up stone not far from there that looks to be a possible cover for such a burial plot. It once belonged to someone from Ireland, which was a point of interest for those who came on the tour.

The cemetery was also once the site of vandalism and neglect. For many years, people used to steal the stones and use them for sidewalks and other various purposes. The city, at one point, allegedly wanted the cemetery to disappear and so they stopped taking care of it. Over time, weeds, bramble, bushes, and trees engulfed it. Wild shrubbery swallowed the graveyard, so people who lived near it didn't even know it was there. The graveyard even became a source of local lore among children, as they would sometimes go in search of it, not knowing where to look.

In the late 90s, the Bullitt County History Museum got together with a local business owner and students from Bullitt Central High School to restore the graveyard. We had some of the former students that worked on the project years ago as guests on the tour. They've confirmed to us how overgrown and busted up the place was when they started work on it. There were broken and missing stones all about the place. It was painfully obvious the town had given up on the Old Pioneer Graveyard.

Once the project was completed, the workers had managed to clear out the bramble and do as much as they could to restore the stones to their proper places. The folks at the museum dug into the archives and created a small memorial marker out front listing all the known burials. However, with the many missing, broken, and faded stones, no one knows the names of everyone interred there.

As we were gathering information for *Jacob Floyd's Shepherdsville History and Haunts Tour*, someone told us the graveyard is allegedly haunted—particularly haunted by doctors who seen wandering amongst the graves at night. Initially, our question was how did they know the ghosts were doctors? Were they dressed as doctors in white coats walking the grounds?

We did eventually hear a story about a young man named Ben Louis Crist, and his father Henry Clay Crist, who were both prominent town doctors in the late 1800s. One afternoon, Ben Crist visited a local druggist by the name of John West after he had apparently said something rude to a lady friend of Ben's. The woman remains anonymous to this day, as the only known information about her is reports referred to her as Miss F. Many think she is a woman by the name of Julia Field.

Upon entering Mr. West's shop, Crist demanded that he apologize to Miss F for whatever he said. West refused, feeling no apology was in order. This led to a heated exchange of words, finally bringing West from behind the counter. As he reached the counter's end, Crist grabbed him by the shirt collar and attempted to draw his gun. West managed to keep the pistol at bay as he grabbed his own. West fired the first shot, which hit his own leg, but then managed to squeeze off two more shots that hit Crist—one in the abdomen and the other in the back.

Ben Crist died the next day—November 16th, 1872. Authorities arrested and charged John West, then released him on a $5000 bail. Four days later, the court acquitted him of all charges. But, what happened next compounds the mystery behind this tale.

A month after the death of his son, Henry Crist suddenly died under mysterious circumstances. Since he was only forty-eight-years-old, this led to speculation over the nature of his demise. While many believed he simply died of a broken heart over the loss of his son—with whom he shared the medical practice—others think there may have been something more sinister at work, and that Henry Crist's death was not what many thought it was.

One story was that after the verdict, Henry vowed revenge. He said no matter what the court decided, he would see the druggist brought to justice. Some believe Henry approached West and tried to make good on his revenge, but West cut him down much in the same way he had Ben. Others think that after hearing this declaration of vengeance, West wasted little time in finding Henry and dispensing of him before the grieving father could take his revenge.

But, that is not all. John West vanished from town not long after this. The man was not native to the county, having apparently come from somewhere in the Georgetown area. He was on no census rolls before or after the shooting. No one knows what actually happened to him, but there are certainly rumors.

While many believed he killed Henry and left town to avoid another trial—one in which he probably believed he would see a conviction—there are others who think his disappearance was not of his own accord. The theory is that he did indeed kill Henry Crist, and that friends of the Crist family found West and exacted the justice upon him they believed he deserved. People of Shepherdsville held the Crists in high regard, and West was rather popular too. But, he was an outsider while the Crists were hometown blood. Some believe because of this, a few men from town put West to death and disposed of his body in an unknown location.

Now, this is simply town legend—with the exception of the actual altercation between Ben and West—but these stories often breed scary tales. Legend has it that on the anniversary of his death, the ghost of Ben Crist walks near his grave. People have also claimed that Henry walks there as well. The father and son are buried side-by-side about midway through the cemetery.

There have also been reports of a white apparition walking along the tree line between the graveyard and Frank E. Simon Park just beyond the land's boundaries. Those who have seen it or heard about it think it might be one of the doctors, since their ghosts wander the grounds.

One evening, while we were stopping by Shepherdsville Pioneer Graveyard for a visit, Jacob remained in the car while Jenny stood by the fence and snapped pictures of the area. Jacob had a camera handy in the car and the sky was turning gray as a storm was rolling in. He began to take pictures of the sky because he liked how the color of the coming storm contrasted with the hue of the sunset. Later on, as Jenny looked through the sky pictures, she saw something small and white hovering near the bushes at the borderline of the park and the graveyard. When zooming it in, we thought it looked like the face of a man with a beard. What was most striking about it was that it appeared in an area blank and dark, without much there to create any illusion to look like this.

Immediately, we decided to return to the graveyard to try to debunk this. Upon arrival, we looked where the anomaly appeared in the photograph. We determined it was not a tombstone, as none in that area was tall enough to reach where the shape had been, and even if they were, none was nearly white enough to match the form. We then decided to walk the bush line and see if any open patches in the shrubbery could have let in any daylight to create the image—there was no such opening; and if there had been, the fact that the day was waning when Jacob took the picture would make it very improbable that this was the answer. One last theory we had was that it could have been a tree, bush, or some other form of shrubbery back there that gave off the impression of a man's face. There was nothing back there to support this theory. Everything in that area was dark and shadowy. Nothing white shone among the shadows. This was an officially unexplained capture.

Naturally, this left us wondering if it was indeed one of the Crists.

One day, after conducting a spirit box session there, we were on our way out. Jenny decided to stop near the marker at the front gate, which listed the known burials in the graveyard. With the device still running, she ran her finger down the names, asked if anyone was there, and could tell her which name her finger was touching. A voice then echoed back, "Henry," and when she looked at where her finger had stopped, it was sitting on Henry Crist. This occurred before we had even heard the tale of the Crists, and after hearing it, we then felt that there was definitely a connection between the incidents.

While the story of Ben and Henry Crist is quite the interesting tale, it is not nearly as mysterious as the other picture we caught in the wooded area behind the graveyard.

On what was one of our first excursions into the graveyard, Jacob caught a very haunting photo. As Jenny was running the spirit box, Jacob walked about the graveyard taking pictures. As he neared the northern edge there at the back of the cemetery, he came to an area where the skeletal trees of autumn stood in the foreground of what looked to be a drainage area. One would have to walk several feet down an embankment to reach it. He found it to be a rather interesting place.

JACOB FLOYD AND JENNY FLOYD

With it being so late in the year, the leaves had fallen, and any movement through there was loud on the still air. As he stood there trying to snap some scenic photos, he heard a heavy trudging noise, as of something large kicking through the leaves. He envisioned either a large dog or deer running through the leaves, or possibly a human walking briskly. The birds in the naked, skinny trees started chirping incessantly. So, just in case he might have been witnessing something unexplained, he started taking pictures. At the time, we had heard the graveyard was haunted, but we hadn't heard the details just yet.

When we went through the pictures later, Jenny found a strange form in the distance. It looks to be a figure in gray—with either gray hair or wearing a gray hood—hunkered down off in the drainage area. We get the impression that it is a woman and her face, which appears to be looking down, is either partially veiled by hair or a shroud.

Once we discovered this image, we returned to the graveyard to debunk it. We searched the entire edge of the area, looking for this very distinct dark shape. We thought maybe there was a fallen tree with roots sticking up that created this form. Or, maybe it was a very gnarly bush, perhaps with garbage caught on it, making that appear to be a person. We also considered the possibility there was a tall pile of rubble, debris, fallen branches, or anything similar that looked like a person. We never saw anything of the sort. We even took more pictures to try to recreate the image. Never saw it again.

Later on, as people approached us with more stories about the graveyard, that was when we heard the tale that there was a settlement back there long ago, before Shepherdsville was established. People have heard the sounds of women's laughter at night, and sometimes soft sobbing, coming from the area beyond the graveyard. They have reported hearing her voice muttering softly in the night, and even seeing the pale apparition of a woman in a dark gown walking among the trees.

Hearing these tales after catching that picture gave us chills, especially since we are often in that graveyard after the sun goes down, conducting our tour by lantern light.

There was one tour late in the year that produced a questionable picture. It was a small tour as the weather was getting colder, and the days much shorter. While Jacob was telling the story of the woman in the ditch area, one of our guests said they heard someone walking through the leaves beyond the trees. He stopped the story and listened, and we heard it as well. Someone then took a picture of the area and it later revealed the image of someone wearing a hat—but it certainly was not Jacob! The form would have been somewhere inside a cluster of trees, and the flash had captured the outline. We never actually saw anyone, and it's quite possible it could have been someone lurking about there at night, but it sure made for an interesting experience, nonetheless.

So, that's the Shepherdsville Pioneer Graveyard and just some of the interesting history and the eerie ghost tales coming out of it. As always, we're not saying that we know the place is haunted, but we can safely say we have had some strange experiences in there, and so have a few of our guests.

JACOB FLOYD AND JENNY FLOYD

Full shot of cemetery with white face

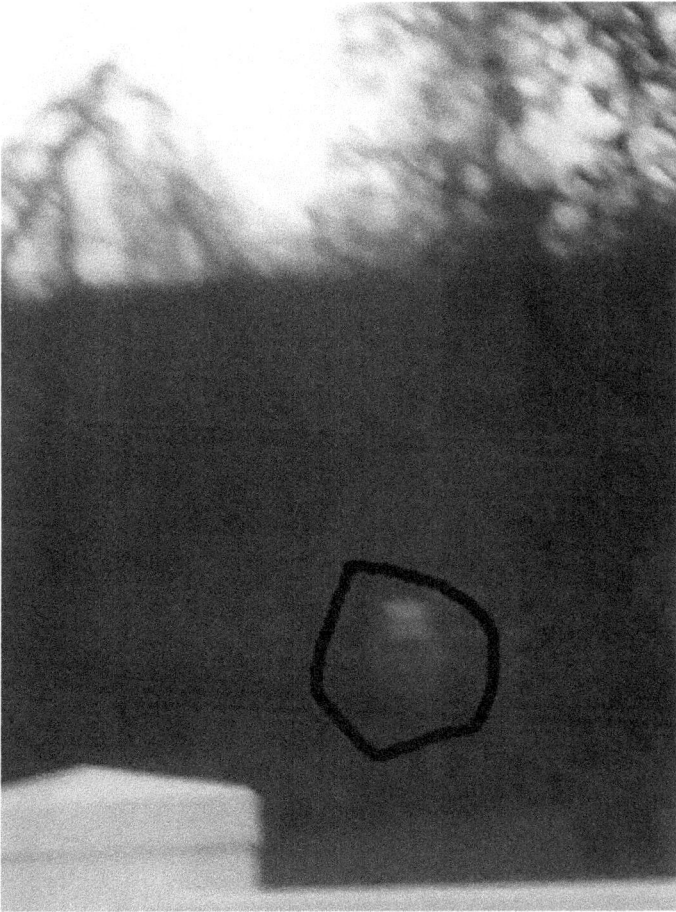

Close up of white face

Area behind graveyard where gray image was spotted

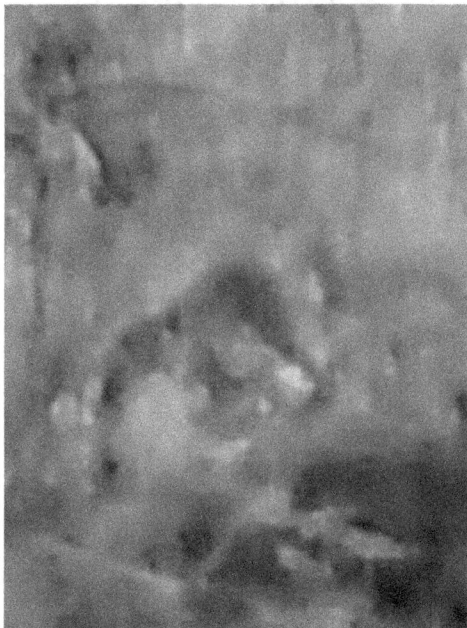

Close up of gray image

JACOB FLOYD AND JENNY FLOYD

THE DARK SECRET
OF A DEAD CEMETERY

Louisville's Strange and Unusual Haunts

KENTUCKY'S HAUNTED GRAVEYARDS

Located next to the sprawling, legendary Cave Hill Cemetery lies the crumbling and forgotten Eastern Cemetery. Spread across only about thirty acres, this cemetery greets you with a rusted, bent, and falling iron fence along with a busted up gate that never closes. From the adjacent sidewalk stretching down the quieter end of Baxter Avenue, anyone passing by can see the unkempt lawn and neglected tombstones and sculptures of old, lonely Eastern Cemetery. Sometimes, a local group of charitable lawn care providers will kindly cut the grass there at no charge, proving that there are those who still care about the history and respect the people buried there.

Though at first glance the grounds appear sad and shabby, even gray and dismal, the further back you go, the more you can come to see the decaying beauty that still clings to the spirit of this place. Anyone with an eye to see beyond the superficial scars the passing years have left can tell that this graveyard was once beautiful and picturesque, much like Cave Hill, only on a smaller scale. Many well-carved decorative statues tower above their markers, though cracked and filthy with careless age, the grime and fractures across the stones only lend credibility to their endurance and character to their faded glory.

In the back stands Louisville's first crematorium, as well as a chapel where the wakes once took place. Due to the vandalism, constant squatting by the homeless, and other desecrations rumored to have taken place there (such as drugs, prostitution, and even Satanic rituals), the old building has been cemented up and put to rest, almost symbolizing the whole landscape as one mass grave—which, sadly, it had been turned into at one point.

JACOB FLOYD AND JENNY FLOYD

Though the exact date of the operation's beginning is not known to us, it appears Eastern was used for burial as far back as the early-1840s, possibly even predating Cave Hill. Once the Eastern Cemetery Corporation formed in the 1850s, they built the crematorium and, in a ghastly turn of events, sold the already filled plots. Reburials began to take place, often times having the previous graves erased and new ones put over top of them. Over the years, the neglect settled in so badly that even as recent as the 1990s, rumors of coffins protruding from the ground circled.

Naturally, with such unseemly events transpiring, and the age passing and decay setting in, stories about specters roaming the grounds have developed. People have reported hearing dogs nearby, seeing them passing in the night, only to vanish behind gravestones and trees. Small groups of shadows huddle in an area that often floods, where the ground is lower and some of the stones tilt.

People who had braved an adventure into the eerie, torn apart chapel back before it was sealed have reported hearing heavy footsteps running in the rooms around them, only to turn their flashlights towards the sounds and see nothing. Shadows and shapes move past the windows, and a sound like chains dragging the floor echoes inside the building.

One person reported what they believe to be something demonic down where the crematory furnaces were. Though no evidence exists to validate this claim, there is a rumor that a small group of Satanists performed Black Mass rituals in the basement. The extent of these alleged rituals are unknown, but visitors to the old building discovered certain sigils and markings, as well as Black Mass items. Some believe the rituals called up something dark and trapped it in the basement. A fast-moving black shape darts about the room, growling and swinging at anyone near. Whenever this dark entity appeared, smoky heat would began to filter slowly from the retired furnaces, causing anyone down below to sweat in the hot stifled air.

On a lighter note, the ghost of a woman tends to the babies' graves behind the old chapel. She is a tall, white, smoky apparition with either long hair or a long veil on, and she appears crossing the grounds towards the back, where she sweeps and cleans the graves of the deceased infants.

We cannot tell you if any of these stories are true, but we can tell you that we are more than willing to believe in the possibility of their existence. If ever there was a place that could test the will of my personal disbelief, other than my mother's house, Eastern Cemetery is the place. Between this quiet burial ground and the homes we lived in growing up, we have no reason to disbelieve, yet still the logic of the limited human mind often prevails. But, when we venture into Eastern Cemetery, that doubt is so often suspended.

We love Eastern Cemetery. It has such a peaceful feel to it, yet you can tell it is teeming with energy. There is a love there, as if those who still exist take pride in their sanctuary. Tension exists upon entrance, but it is not frightful—until you get back to the closed-up chapel. Though the view from the front steps of the building is a breathtaking panoramic scope of the storied grounds, it does feel like a turbulent dark energy pulsates behind the cement. It could just be the residual energy left from years of foul play that took place within, or maybe energy from all the overpopulated graves, or maybe just the stigma of negativity people often associate with the unusual history. Either way, a sensitive will certainly feel something peculiar upon entering.

During one of our first visits there, we caught a picture of a white form floating through the same section of the graveyard where the gathering of shadows appears. The figure appears white and somewhat blocky. While we can see there is something paranormal crossing the grass, it's hard to say what it is. However, a few people whom we have shown the picture to have said it looks like a woman with a long veil atop her head, which strikes me odd due to the story of the white, feminine manifestation that has been seen tending to the infants' graves. While she mostly walks the area behind the old crematory, it is still possible for her to travel the cemetery at will.

In the same section where we caught this shape, we had one of our strangest experiences. If indeed shadows congregate in this area, I believe we saw one with our own eyes. Unlike with the feminine form, which we only noticed after reviewing pictures, we actually witnessed this happening not long after we pulled to the spot and stopped. Jenny told me she saw what looked like a torso moving around the trees. It was a bright sunny afternoon and we were supposed to meet someone there. But, on the off chance that it was someone up to no good, or the man we were supposed to meet, Jacob decided to get out and look before we commenced our investigation.

As Jacob headed in the direction Jenny pointed, he stopped in his tracks. From behind one of the high standing tombstones, about fifteen feet away, he saw a dark form emerge and shoot quickly from the stone to behind a large tree a few feet to the right. Both the speed and the manner in which it moved was unnatural: it raised up, in a slight arch, and came back down behind the tree very quickly; it was about the size of a human, but I did not see leg movement, nor did the form stretch all the way to the ground as if it had legs.

Not wanting to miss an opportunity for some good evidence, I ran back to the car, got our video camera and spirit box and began filming as I tried to not only spot it, but make contact with it, as well. I was not able to do either. I walked directly to where I had seen it, and traveled the entire grounds around that section and never saw it again—and I never saw anyone in the graveyard, either. I also got my digital recorder and started asking questions, but upon review, I had no responses.

Maybe I could chalk that up to someone else being there that we simply didn't see. But, another visit turned out an incident even more harrowing. As we were driving out one day after taking some pictures, we stopped on the last stretch of road towards the exit. Jenny said she saw something dark moving among the trees and stones on the northern side of the cemetery. She began to take pictures. Jacob looked over to the spot she was photographing and saw a dark, circular ball move about the tree branches. We thought it could be anything. Then we saw it a second time, moving back towards where it came from when we first saw it. The breeze momentarily blew aside the branches, exposing the brownish orb against the backdrop of light-colored buildings beyond the Eastern fence line. But, the branches fell back into place and it was gone, again. Then, one more time, I saw it descend towards the ground only to move back up and off to the right, vanishing into the trees. The paranormal rarely moves Jacob, but this one gave him chills. When Jenny reviewed her pictures later, she found that she did in fact catch a semi-transparent dark orb hovering in that area.

Eastern Cemetery is haunted. I have almost no doubt about that; and, this is not something you'll hear me say with such certainty about many other places. The only question, in my mind, that can truly exist is what a haunt is. If it consists of spirits from the afterlife, or something else, I don't know. But, whatever it is, it is in Eastern Cemetery, and it's not afraid to reveal itself.

HIDDEN At THE zoo

JACOB FLOYD AND JENNY FLOYD

The Louisville Zoo, located at 1100 Trevilian Way in the city's Poplar Level neighborhood, opened in May 0f 1969. The zoo stands on the former land of Ben Collins, from whom the city acquired the land a few years prior. Hosting a number of exhibits—such as gorilla enclosures, Wallaroo Walkabout, and Glacier Run—the Louisville Zoo has remained one of the city's premier attractions, bringing in anywhere from 700,000 to almost a million visitors annually.

There are over 1,200 animals housed at the zoo. African lions, Asian elephants, western lowland gorillas, giraffes, the southern white rhinoceros, and a plethora of birds, amphibians, fish, and reptiles are among the many species you can view venturing around the compound. Over the years, there have been some particularly noteworthy animals. An African elephant named Scotty, who was the first elephant born in Kentucky, was there from its birth in 2007 until its sudden death from gastrointestinal disorders in 2010. A Masai giraffe named Bakari born with an angular limb deformity, was believed to be the first of its species to ever have a periosteal stripping performed on its leg, resides at the zoo. Thelma, the first-known reticulated python to give birth without a mate while in captivity, did so there in 2014. Former NASCAR Cup Series champion Tony Stewart donated his pet patas monkey, Mojo, to the zoo in 2007 after it became too aggressive. Perhaps the most famous of all—at least to the locals—is Qannik, the orphaned Polar bear found in the Alaskan Northern Slope in 2011, who came to live at Glacier Run after the exhibit was completed.

Outside of a couple of incidents of animals thought to have escaped, only to be found hiding not far from their enclosures, there have been a few incidents at the Louisville Zoo everyone would like to forget—the most recent being the zoo train derailment of 2009. The passenger car toppled over after the engine and three open-air cars went off the track. The driver at the time was inexperienced and had gone too fast when rounding a curve. This injured twenty-two passengers, resulting in some lawsuits. It took six years to close those suits, and the train reopened. However, in 2019, after a partial mine collapse at the nearby Mega Cavern, a sinkhole was found near the train, and thus the attraction was closed. The zoo auctioned off the new trains, with one going to the Fort Worth Zoo in Fort Worth, Texas, and the other staying right here in Kentucky at the allegedly haunted Buffalo Trace Distillery in the state capitol of Frankfort.

Another horrifying incident occurred back in 1994 when Kenya, an African elephant, decided she wanted to have some fun with one of the patrons. Kenya was normally docile, but on this day, she wanted to play. After having just given rides to some of the customers, Kenya wandered over to the man, picked him up with her trunk, and proceeded to drop him. She did this several times, injuring the man to the point where he had to have his spleen and a portion of his pancreas removed.

These are not the only strange and interesting aspects about the zoo. There is also a small gravesite located on the property. Many people don't even know about it. Visitors may frequent the Louisville Zoo and walk right past it, never once noticing.

The gravesite is a simple plot surrounded by a modest wall made of stone, with a thin iron gateway. This is the

JACOB FLOYD AND JENNY FLOYD

Phillips-Durrett-Clark Cemetery, named for those related to the man interred there, named Jenkins Phillips.

According to record, as well as the etchings on the stone, Phillips was a private in the Virginia Militia during the Revolutionary War, and had fought alongside George Washington. It is also stated he surveyed much of Kentucky for Henry Clay, who played a sizeable role in the history of Kentucky as well; and, whose mansion – Ashland – is reported to be haunted, and was featured in our book *Kentucky's Haunted Mansions*.

Jenkins Phillips lived 1744-1822. Other members of the Phillips family listed on the marker at the Louisville Zoo are Thomas, Sallie, Lydia B., Richard, Samuel (1834-1853), Samuel (1797-1854), Joanna, Hannah Allen, and Hanna DuBerley Phillips. Other named on the stone are Darius Hamilton, Lydia Clark, and Virginia Riley.

Why is this cemetery at the zoo? Well, the cemetery was there first. Workers building the zoo discovered the cemetery during construction. Since there was still a living relative who might use the plot, the owners of the zoo respected the sacred ground and opted not to relocate the cemetery, but to build the attraction around it, instead.

Is it haunted? Well, not to our knowledge. We've never heard stories about any ghosts or strange occurrences, nor could we find any online. But, it is certainly interesting, and so we thought it would be an interesting inclusion.

A WITCH AND
HER WATCHER

Kentucky's Strange and Unusual Haunts

Pilot's Knob is a small cemetery off Ford's Ferry Road in Marion. Home to a lot of greenery and timeworn tombstones, there is one grave that has gathered quite of bit of notoriety from local paranormal enthusiasts. That is the burial site of young Mary Evelyn Ford.

Rumor was that Mary was a child witch, daughter of a witch, and the townsfolk looked upon her and her mother with disdain and fear. What crimes the child and her mother had committed that created such a suspicion is unknown, but without a trial, people in town deemed them practitioners of the dark arts and sentenced them to death by fire sometime in the 1910s. Mary, who was only about six years old at the time, would suffer the same fate as her mother.

The people in the community held a great fear that Mary Evelyn would travel to the void and, from there, begin casting spells against the town. So, they lined her grave with steel, interred her into the ground at Pilot's Knob, and placed rocks upon her grave. Why they thought such precautions would keep the forces of darkness at bay is hard to say. But so is why they believed Mary Evelyn and her mother to be witches. For extra measure, they built a picket fence around the plot out of crosses that connect end-to-end; probably believing the forces of light would repel any wickedness the poor child's witchy soul would cast their way.

JACOB FLOYD AND JENNY FLOYD

To take the superstitious nature of the entire tale even further, people have claimed there is a watcher who stands sentinel by Mary's grave, attempting to get to the girl and free her supposedly sinister spirit, either to help her or so it can take her soul. However, the cross fence is believed to form a spiritual barrier that keeps the watcher from completing its duties. No one knows what this watcher is or where it comes from, but some believe it could be the soul of one of the witch's victims.

According to some, though, the girl's restless spirit is not in captivity. They say that she can be seen walking the confines of her plot, stuck between the crosses, but still able to drain anyone in the graveyard of energy in order to make herself stronger. She entices people to pass the fence and come into her tiny prison. She does this by making faces at her prey, and when they come into her domain, she will pull them into her grave.

That's a wild assertion, but there are other paranormal accounts. A group of college kids alleged to have seen tiny footprints atop Mary's grave. As they approached to get a closer look, the infamous watcher chased them from the area.

One couple claimed to have heard the sound of a young girl laughing in the cemetery at night. They followed the laughter to Mary's grave and claimed they saw a shadowy presence moving near the fence. Fearing it was actually a human lurking in the darkness, they left.

Other folks have reported laughter, as well. They have also alleged to hear voices in the cemetery. People interested in checking out the legend have also reported being touched on the lower back. One person said they were touched on the back and had a small, pink handprint where they felt the touch the following day. Many report an eerie feeling in the cemetery, but that could be due to the legends, as well as the seclusion of the location.

While the story of Mary and her mother is quite spooky, it is not accurate at all. According to Mary's death certificate, she died in 1916 from peritonitis and rectal impaction, not burning, and was five at the time of her death, not six. She was the daughter of Mary Rebecca Davis and James Ford. Rebecca outlived Mary, passing away in 1955. It seems as though this tale is a complete fabrication.

That, however, does not mean the reported paranormal activity is a hoax. Perhaps the activity happened first, and people made up the story to explain it. The area has close connections to the Civil War, and we know how often those locations are hotbeds of paranormal reports. If there truly is anything supernatural lingering in Pilot's Knob Cemetery, it could very well be from that.

Unless the countless times people have told the tale of young Mary the witch has caused her spirit some unrest, and she's actually back to silence the lies.

As for the Watcher, there is a tale of someone hanged from or murdered on a swinging bridge near the cemetery. Legend also has it that spirits of those robbed and murdered by river pirate James Ford and his Ford's Ferry Gang haunt nearby Ford's Ferry.

To the public eye, James Ford, born in 1775 in the then Province of South Carolina, British America, was a Pillar of the Community. A civic leader, militiaman, owner of multiple properties, and successful business owner across western Kentucky and southern Illinois, Ford presented a stellar image. But, at the time, people didn't know the illicit activities he was partaking in that would one day earn him the nickname, Satan's Ferryman.

Through his connections in Illinois, Ford befriended vicious highwayman Isiah Potts, head of the of the notorious Pott's Hill Gang. There he also came to know the illegal slave trader John Hart Crenshaw. Once he settled on the Kentucky side of the Ohio, he might have fallen in with Samuel Mason's river pirates, who operated out of Cave-in-Rock just on the other side of the Ohio River from Crittenden County in Kentucky. This is whereabouts the ferry was located. Other associates of Ford's were the family of counterfeiters known as the Sturdivant Gang, whom he helped move counterfeit money into Illinois.

Ford was cruel and ruthless. He not only tortured his slaves, but was also heavily involved with the Reverse Underground Railroad in the area, kidnapping freemen and runaway slaves for illegal trade. The road from the house of John Hart Crenshaw leading to Ford's Ferry was a much-used path on the Railroad.

His gang robbed flatboats using the Ohio River to come into the area. Story tells they murdered many people during that time. This bloody criminal activity is likely the cause of paranormal activity in the area.

On July 7th, 1833, members of his gang ambushed Ford at his home near Ford's Ferry and shot him dead. Their identities and motives remain unknown. Some believe it was an act of vigilantism. Perhaps, it could have been a "hit" of some kind. Proverbially, Ford led two lives: one of stand-up citizenship, and the other as a ferocious criminal with no concern for human life. It is possible, somewhere in between the two worlds, someone decided it was time to remove him. Maybe they feared his public notoriety would eventually lead to their exposure; or, maybe he just crossed the wrong person along the way.

So, who is the menacing Watcher haunting Pilot's Knob? Is it James Ford? Not likely. Ford's grave lies in the Ford Family Cemetery in Tolu, Kentucky close to twenty miles northwest of Pilot's Knob. But Ford's Ferry was only about ten miles from the cemetery. Is it possible someone murdered there has found their way into Pilot Knob? Maybe one of the gang members' spirits are there, keeping watch like they used to while the gang was carrying out their criminal activities.

We wonder if Mary Evelyn Ford is a relation of James Ford. We have reached out to historians local to the area, and have received no reply. We have also searched through records to make a connection, but have been unsuccessful in finding any extensive documentation to answer this question. Given the close proximity, it is certainly a possibility there is a relation between Mary Evelyn and James Ford, even if it is distant. However, since Ford is a common surname, it is possible there is no direct connection.

JACOB FLOYD AND JENNY FLOYD

THE OLD PIONEER CEMETERY

Kentucky's Strange and Unusual Haunts

KENTUCKY'S HAUNTED GRAVEYARDS

The Old Pioneer Cemetery in Bardstown lies behind another location reported to be quite haunted – The Talbott Tavern. Nearby, the Jailer's Inn, which is a former jail turned bed and breakfast, is supposedly haunted. These three locations are right next to each other in the historic district of Bardstown, which both Rand McNally and *USA Today* named one of the nicest small towns in America.

Some years back, a ghost hunter by the name of Patti Starr used to conduct a tour of all three locations, where she would use photography and digital recordings to attempt to capture any electronic voice phenomena, or pictures of spirits in the area. We took the tour many years ago. During which, it was believed Starr caught an apparition in a photograph, and a possible voice on her digital recorder. Whether she did or not, we cannot say. They were interesting bits of evidence.

There are many alleged paranormal encounters at the Old Talbott Tavern. The most common includes orbs and lights seen hovering throughout the tavern. Many investigators have photographed these occurrences. Employees and guests have seen a ghostly lady in white in the tavern. Guests have woken up to her hovering beside the bed, only to turn around and float from the room when spotted. This has caused the guests to leave early. Others have seen shadow figures emerging from dark corners walk into the light and vanish.

One night, a bookkeeper and a cook saw a man in a long black coat on the top landing when no one else was supposed to be in the building. The man turned and walked away with the employees trailing him through several rooms. Eventually, the man walked through the fire escape door. Upon opening the door, the employees saw the man on the landing, staring at them. He then emitted a maniacal laugh and vanished in front of them.

A few weeks later, the bookkeeper and her husband were watching a special on television. The show was about Jesse James. When his picture flashed upon the screen, she grabbed her husband's arm and said, "Oh my God – that is the same face I saw the other night that disappeared." Employees have named this ghost Jesse James, for he has appeared on a number of occasions. There is no record of James ever having come to Bardstown, KY, but the legend people tell around the Old Talbott Tavern is that he did once stay there and shot holes in the wall somewhere to mark his stay. This alleged wall burned in a fire that occurred at the Tavern many years ago.

Furniture moves on its own, actively jumping and sliding in front of witnesses. Utensils, like forks and spoons, fly from tables and skid along the floor, sometimes landing atop the mantle of the fireplace where employees have found them. Room keys vanish from the front desk only to have staff find them lying in one of the hallways later.

People often hear phantom footsteps in empty rooms and corridors; doors slam in the middle of the night; guests hear mysterious raps on their doors when no one is there; and disembodied voices speak from empty rooms. On top of these common happenings, strange music has been heard playing in certain rooms without anyone present and no radios nor televisions playing. Chimes from unidentified clocks ring out in the small hours of the night, with no chimes occurring during the daylight hours. An old piano in the building often plays by itself.

We stayed at the Talbott Tavern overnight many years back, attempting a paranormal investigation. There wasn't a whole lot that transpired, but we did get some activity in the conference room on the second floor. While in there operating our spirit box, we heard a loud whistle inside the room right after we turned off the box. There was no one else in the room with us. Jacob quickly left the room to see if anyone was out on the floor. No one was there. While it is possible someone could have passed by the room and whistled directly by the door, the upstairs is so unstable that people hear and feel any footsteps on the main floor. If someone had walked by, they would have had to go down the stairs—which we would have heard—or have gone into a room—which we also would have heard—before they could be out of sight.

Before we left the conference room behind for good, Jacob stood just outside the door, taking pictures and using the digital recorder. During this time, he heard footsteps passing through the room, causing the floor to creak. Again, as we said, footsteps on the second floor of the Talbott Tavern echo and shake all around. However, there was no one else walking by at the time, and the creaks coming from inside the room aligned with the creaks, which could be heard when someone actively crosses the floor in the conference room.

Townsfolk say the Jailer's Inn next door to the Talbott Tavern is haunted. The property has been the site of the Old Nelson County Jail since 1797, with the current jail constructed in 1814. The addition in the back came in 1874. Hangings used to occur in the yard behind the jail. In 1987, the jail shut down. After an auction in 1989, the building became the Jailer's Inn Bed and Breakfast.

JACOB FLOYD AND JENNY FLOYD

Most of the haunts you hear about coming from the Jailer's Inn involve the old cellblock in the back of the building. Word is that footsteps travel up and down the stairs at night, walking the cellblock, and the doors to the cells slam shut. Guests can stay in what used to be the women's cell, located just outside the cellblock. That is where we stayed when we decided to investigate the Jailer's Inn. We didn't experience much of anything. Our spirit box session yielded no results, neither did the digital recorder. Nothing turned up in photos or on video, either. While we slept, we did hear footsteps on the stairs accompanied by the sound of slamming doors. We didn't think anything of it, however, because the innkeeper lives at the top of those stairs, and we assume it was her walking up and down them. The door slamming, we also determined, was the door to her rooms at the top of the stairs.

The Old Pioneer Cemetery located behind the Jailer's Inn has some historic significance. Some graves there date back to the 1700s. The man who invented the steamboat—John Fitch—was, at one time, interred there. Some of the prisoners hanged at the old jail allegedly rest there as well.

Most of the tales of hauntings involve apparitions and unexplainable sounds. People have caught pictures of mysterious orbs, but orbs are highly controversial as many can be dust or bugs. The dark shape of a man passes through the cemetery late at night. Some say he follows people until they leave the grounds.

When we visited the graveyard, we didn't have many experiences except for a few possible responses on the spirit box. We thought we saw a shadow passing behind one of the chest tombs, but could not be certain. We were not able to capture it in a photo. Though, someone we spoke to there did report watching a shape rise from behind a corner grave, walk across the cemetery grounds, and vanish just before the edge at the other side.

With all the history, energy, and alleged hauntings transpiring around the area, between the Talbott Tavern and the Jailer's Inn, it's no wonder there might be some spirits wandering about the Old Pioneer Cemetery out back. If nothing else, these are all very interesting historical locations to visit. So, if you're ever near Bardstown, we recommend stopping in for a bit.

JACOB FLOYD AND JENNY FLOYD

THE CHAPEL

Kentucky's Strange and Unusual Haunts

KENTUCKY'S HAUNTED GRAVEYARDS

Judge Mason Brown created the Frankfort Cemetery, located in the state capital of Frankfort, on February 27th, 1844. The cemetery is the burial ground for eighteen former Kentucky governors, as well as many other former politicians. Other notable people interred there are the escape artist Gilbert Genesta, poet Theodore O'Hara, sculptor Joel Tanner Hart, artist Paul Sawyier, and professional wrestling manager Elizabeth Ann Hulette, also known as Miss Elizabeth. The most famous person buried at Frankfort Cemetery is folk hero and frontiersman, the American pioneer Daniel Boone.

The cemetery is beautiful, and has a breathtaking view of the city over one of the ledges looking down the hillside. Many trees and other forms of shrubbery taken from the mountains of Kentucky populate the graveyard. The design is in the Romanesque architectural style, with many terraces, curving lanes, and circles of vaults across the grounds. The Frankfort Cemetery is quite a remarkable sight, and a nice place for a peaceful stroll.

That is unless you are one among the many of individuals to witness any of the perceived paranormal events reported to have transpired there. Over the years, many people have claimed to experience some spooky encounters while visiting Frankfort Cemetery. Many, of course, come to see the gravesite of Daniel Boone, but they often get more than they expected.

Those walking the grounds on peaceful afternoons and even into the evening have reported the silence broken by laughter coming from someone unseen. Shadow figures move past trees and around tombstone. Others have even reported a child running through the cemetery. People will see this child passing by, call to him, and even follow in hopes of seeing if he is lost and needs help finding his parents. Before they can catch him, he'll dart behind a tree and not return.

Perhaps the most haunted piece of the cemetery is the chapel. Built in 1890, the chapel stands upon the cliff overlooking the city. Pre-burial funeral services took place there until 1932. After that, it became a storage facility. In 1977 and 78, the interior of the building underwent repair work and renovation; in 2003, exterior repairs followed. Visitors can now enter the chapel.

Some of those who have explored the chapel have reported feeling very uneasy—even sick—at times, as if someone is watching them, something not so friendly. Whispering voices drift through the inside when no one else was present other than the visitors. Here is where another large shadow figure often stands in the corner, or crosses the floor. The form is tall, dark, and carries an ominous vibe. Those who have seen this figure, or felt its presence, have left the building immediately.

Upon out visit there, we did experience a few strange occurrences. While we didn't see the child, we thought we heard something similar to a child crying. Not bawling, but merely sobbing, or making some noise like it. We looked about, but saw no child, nor anyone else who could have made that noise. We thought maybe it was an unidentified animal of some kind and continued our exploration.

There was a strange door open in a hillside, and Jacob joked that it was Bag End, the home of Bilbo Baggins, and asked, "Are we in the Shire?" We are not entirely certain what the door led to—we assume some sort of maintenance tunnel or tool shed—but, we did decide to investigate, out of curiosity. We were several yards away when we heard something like a low howl coming from the area. We stopped and looked at each other. Then we heard it a little louder. There was a loud scuffing sound, as if someone had banged into something near the hole in the hillside, just before the door slammed shut. We decided not to investigate further.

When Jenny saw the chapel, she became instantly uneasy. Jacob wanted to look in, but Jenny was very apprehensive. As they drew nearer, she told Jacob she did not want to go in there. When he asked why, she said she felt something—like bad energy—coming from within; the feeling got so strong she started to feel sick. Jacob said he would go check it out himself, and she urged him not to. A few seconds later, they both saw a figure come into view beyond the windows. From where we stood, neither of us could discern exact details, but the figure looked like a large dark shape of a man without any defining features. At this point, even Jacob could feel the presence. Jenny said it was time to leave. She no longer wanted to stay in Frankfort Cemetery.

Of course, we cannot say what we saw inside the chapel was a spirit of any kind. What we can say is that we had not heard the ghost stories of the cemetery prior to our visit, so the reports of the shadow figure were unknown to us. It wasn't until after experiencing the creepy moments there that we decided to research to see if the cemetery was haunted. When someone told us of the figure in the chapel, we decided that very well could have been what we saw. However, it could have easily been a man there in the chapel.

JACOB FLOYD AND JENNY FLOYD

MINNIE'S GONE MISSING

Located just down the road from North Bullitt High School and Hebron Middle School in northern Bullitt County is the small, but nice, Hebron Cemetery. Developed in 1894, Hebron Cemetery replaced the Old Pioneer Graveyard, or as we dubbed, the Forgotten Cemetery, from our book *Kentucky's Strange and Unusual Haunts*, as well as featured in the final chapter of this book.

There are many people significant to Bullitt County history interred at Hebron Cemetery. However, the best-known person laid to rest there is actor, artist, and author Gardner McKay. Though McKay was born in New York City and died in Hawaii, he stayed a while in the Louisville area as his father and grandfather were from Covington, Shelbyville, and Louisville. Other family members of his had lived in both Bullitt and Nelson counties.

A Revolutionary War soldier named John Beckwith rests at Hebron Cemetery. He was the one who thought of building the old schoolhouse that once stood near to the graveyard. Beckwith's original grave was in the Old Brooks Cemetery, later sold and relocated. The city moved Beckwith's body, along with those of his family, and their stones, to the Hebron Cemetery.

We have heard conflicting reports regarding Beckwith. Many articles and historical records state he is buried there. Some historians believe his body isn't actually there, just the stone, and that his body remains where the Brooks Cemetery was, which now has U of L Medical Center South standing on top of it. We do not know for certain, but we have visited the graves. They are very close together, so it's possible no one is actually in any of the Beckwith graves. It's also not hard to believe the city buried them close together and had the stones simply placed on top of the site, maybe not necessarily spaced out precisely.

As for haunts, there is a story of a woman who wanders around the graveyard at night, carrying a lantern among the rows of tombstones, looking to the trees for her cat. The woman is elderly, dressed in a long black dress and apron, with a covering over her head, as if protecting herself from a cold wind that blew the night she lost her pet. Some say she appears only on a night when the moon is full and bright in the sky, as an apparition in the moonlight. Others say she appears only for a few nights around Halloween, leaving people to believe this is why she appears in such attire. There are more conflicting accounts of her appearances, as some say she has appeared on random nights throughout the years. There are those who have reported seeing her at dusk, just as the sun slips behind the horizon; others say she appears right around midnight; lastly, her arrival allegedly coincides with three in the morning. If all of this is accurate, this leads us to believe she truly appears at various times.

As the story goes, the woman is seen somewhere near the center of the cemetery, her lantern light bobbing ominously in the darkness, moving towards the south end of the graveyard, gazing up into the sky, and into nearby trees, yelling for her cat. Some believe when she appears to be simply looking to the sky, her spirit is actually checking in trees that were there when she had searched for her beloved feline companion, but are no longer there now. She will search for a few minutes, calling her cat's name, before becoming frantic with concern that she will not find her pet.

There are those who have seen her searching and have approached her to help. Some accounts say she ignores them when they ask her if she's okay or needs help. She just keeps yelling, "Minnie! Minnie where are you?" Witnesses have followed her for a few minutes, only for her to disappear into the shadows of the night.

Another story claims the lady will answer. This one is from where, we think, the description of her being elderly came. In this account, the witness approaches her and asks if she is okay. Instead of ignoring the other person, the woman turns to them, takes down her head covering, and says, "I'm looking for cat Minnie. Have you seen a black cat around here?" Once the person tells her no, the woman resumes her search and vanishes.

There have been reports of a light floating through the graveyard, and near the trees, without the presence of the woman. The light is large, orb-like, but with small beams radiating from the center. It travels around the center of the cemetery to the south end before vanishing. We suspect this happens when the woman's apparition cannot fully form, but the light is still present.

Minnie, it seems, might actually be present in Hebron Cemetery. People have reported hearing a disembodied cat meow towards the center of the cemetery, even possibly in the trees. The cat meows are somewhat urgent, but none can see the cat.

There have also been reports of a black cat seen walking across tombstones in the center of the cemetery. When approached, she meows, jumps down, and vanishes. There is a tale that Minnie runs from behind the stone towards the south end of the cemetery, disappearing in the sea of tombstones.

A black cat walks across the fence at the southern end of Hebron Cemetery. Whenever someone shines their flashlight on it, it looks towards them, meows, and vanishes. Another story places Minnie in a tree at the center of the graveyard. Someone wandering the paths will hear a meow, look up, and see the black cat there in the tree. If they look away for a second, the cat will be gone when they look back, never to be seen climbing down the tree, on any other branches, or down on the ground near the tree.

Of course, it's easy to explain these occurrences with the cat. It's a black cat in a graveyard at nighttime, surrounded by tombstones and trees. It could easily flee without notice. The cat could hide behind the stones, climb higher into the trees, or run away so swiftly no one spots it before it finds a crevice in which it can squeeze.

There is one story, though, much more difficult to explain. A couple who were visiting the grave of a family member, and there to see the Revolutionary War graves, said they were there close to sundown. As they approached the middle of the graveyard, they heard a cat meowing, as if in need of help. They looked around for a few minutes, unable to find it, even though it kept meowing. Eventually, they saw it in a tree. The woman called to the cat, but it wouldn't come down. They decided it must be okay, so they went to leave, as it was getting dark.

As they were leaving the cemetery, they heard a meow behind them. They turned to see the cat following them to their car, parked close to the entrance. The woman moved to pick the cat up, but it backed away, so she went towards the car.

When she sat down, the cat came up to her and meowed. So, she let it jump on her lap. She asked her fiancé if they could take the cat home, since it didn't have a collar or anything indicating it was someone's pet. Reluctantly, he agreed. As they drove towards the exit, the cat became apprehensive and meowed, with its eyes wide. Just as they were about to pass through the exit, the cat meowed again and suddenly jumped into the backseat. When the woman turned around to see what it was doing, the cat was no longer there. The back windows were down, so she wondered if it jumped through one. Watching as they drove away to see if she saw it, she never did.

As it turns out, the woman, at the time, was wearing a long black skirt. We wonder if the cat was Minnie, and thought she had found her owner. This would be why she followed the couple and jumped on the woman's lap. Perhaps, once she realized it wasn't her owner, she decided to jump out and go back to Hebron Cemetery to wait for her. Maybe, Minnie is bound to the cemetery and cannot leave, and that's why she exited the vehicle as it passed through the exit. Of course, it could have been just a stray cat. As anyone who has spent any significant time around cats knows, they are capable of moving in some very erratic ways.

GHOSTS IN THE BELL

Kentucky's Strange and Unusual Haunts

Established in 1848, the Lexington Cemetery was created to help deal with the high number of bodies that needed burying due to the area's cholera epidemic. It began as forty acres but has since expanded to 170, with more than 64,000 buried there. The cemetery has three listings on the National Register of Historic Places, including the Ladies' Confederate Memorial, the Confederate Soldier Monument, and the Lexington National Cemetery. There are a myriad of tree species around the land. There is an American basswood, which staff claim is the largest in the world, although the National Register of Big Trees says the largest American basswood is in Pennsylvania.

There are a number of notable individuals buried there. Among them are Jim Varney, Phyllis George, Adolph Rupp, John Young Brown, Jr., Ralph Wesley Foody, Gay Brewer, C.M. Newton, James Lane Allen, Gene Markey, Sarah Gibson Humphreys, Joseph Henry Bush, and Vernon Hatton. Many prominent Kentucky politicians, architects, activists, and academics are interred in Lexington Cemetery, as well.

Among these noteworthy names, there are reportedly many ghosts roaming the cemetery grounds. Misty apparitions have taken form in various locations, floating from one area to the next. The air around them grows chill, even on warm days. Unintelligible whispers accompany them as they pass. Witnesses report seeing more than one at a time, and watching them sometimes come together.

KENTUCKY'S HAUNTED GRAVEYARDS

In a more harrowing account, shadow figures drift around tombstones, bringing a sense of dread at their approach. People have reported hearing their footsteps swishing through the grass and clacking on the roads leading through the graveyard. They appear from nowhere, and disappear as quickly from sight.

The most frightening spot in Lexington Cemetery is the Bell Mausoleum, which was dedicated on October 23rd, 1974. Visitors report seeing more shadow figures walking towards and around the back of the mausoleum. Sounds of shrill laughter, desperate screams, disembodied voices, and heavy knocks and thumps from within the structure have scared many witnesses.

Those who have gotten too close to the mausoleum at the wrong times smelled an aroma often described as rot and decay; other times, people insist it's Sulphur. There is a sewage treatment plant nearby, which could explain the odor. However, that does not explain the feelings of intense anger that overcome some people who stand near the Bell Mausoleum and see a large black shadow step around the structure. Some who have experienced this rage describe it as a feeling of destruction, and even with murderous intentions. People overtaken by this sensation feel sudden urges towards violence. Once they are away from the mausoleum, and the feeling subsides, the onset of fear and waves of nausea seize them.

Since we first wrote about Lexington Cemetery in *Kentucky's Strange and Unusual Haunts*, we have revisited the cemetery a time or two. Prior to the original publication, we didn't have any experiences. Since returning, we *have* seen misty apparitions passing among the gravestones. We also heard voices talking somewhere towards the center of the cemetery without seeing any other visitors. When approaching the Bell Mausoleum, we did not see any shadowy figures, but we did hear something that sounded like thumping inside the building. No feelings of anger, dread, or sickness came upon us, but we definitely felt some sort of energy nearby.

We do plan to revisit Lexington Cemetery at some point in hopes of seeing something else. We heard rumors of a coven of witches having spent time in the cemetery at one point, and the alleged sighting of a Bigfoot nearby and on the grounds. Further research into these claims yielded no additional information. Maybe one day, we'll hear more.

THE GATES OF HELL
Kentucky's Strange and Unusual Haunts

Grandview Cemetery, also known as Kasey Cemetery, is a hard-to-find graveyard buried deep in the woods of Custer, Kentucky. Though many say it is in Elizabethtown, it is actually about twenty miles west of town. To find it, you must head northwest on a windy dirt path known as St. John's Road. It is very secluded, located in a rather peaceful clearing in the woods, surrounded by the ruins of a stone and iron gate. Once you find its broken remains, according to legend, you will have found the Gates of Hell.

Before Grandview had such an ominous moniker, it was simply a small-town cemetery for families dating back to the 1700s, giving it a three-hundred-plus-year history in which any number of tragic events could have taken place to pin spirits to the grounds. The nickname the "Gates of Hell" is more than thirty years old, and at one point, people called the cemetery the "killing field." There were reported signs of devil worship found on the premises, particularly animal sacrifices. People have reported seeing charred animal bones throughout Grandview.

In April of 2003, two members of the Kentucky Society for Ghost Research were investigating the graveyard when they came upon the scattered remains of three dogs, two cats, a deer, a calf, and a puppy. The investigators insisted ties to satanic rituals was the cause, and claimed that every time they visit Grandview, they find black candles and occult images drawn in various places. But, after they notified the authorities, the police found nothing to tie the cruelty to anything ritualistic, finding neither black candles nor satanic markings, and the only graffiti they found were swastikas, a body outline, and an orange-yellow image of a cross, none of which are satanic. There have been reports of figures in dark robes kneeling and praying near the graveyard, which could lend credence to the claims of Satanism. But, satanic rituals or not, the graveyard has been heavily vandalized over the years and the tombstones desecrated, which could be the reason for any restless spirits that might be drifting about the Gates of Hell.

Some visitors have experienced severe car troubles after parking outside the cemetery. Batteries have died and cars have refused to start. People have even reported finding personal items inside their cars moved and rearranged.

Automobile difficulties are not the only mechanical malfunctions to occur. Investigators have had newly charged and replaced batteries in their equipment die almost instantly upon entering the graveyard. Others have reported videos with sound and no picture, and cell phones going from full life to dead in a matter of seconds. GPS devices go haywire near the cemetery, only to return to normal once the vehicle has pulled out of the vicinity.

Investigators and those who have traveled to the Gates of Hell out of sheer curiosity have felt a crushing sense of dread, as if something wicked were right upon their backs. They have said they felt as though evil eyes were upon them, watching every move they made. This feeling often becomes so overpowering that those suffering from it have felt suddenly sick and had to leave.

Supposedly, an enormous bright-green orb hovers around the graveyard. Those encountering this strange anomaly say that it hovers in place for a few seconds, then races around the cemetery before rising into the sky and vanishing, or zipping into the woods, out of sight. There are stories about people chased from the cemetery by this peculiar light. One legend tells of a time when the orb appeared over the gate, hovering for quite some time. Some believe its presence caused the gate to bend and break, and the stones to crumble, and this is the reason for the gate's destruction.

What may have given rise to the Gates of Hell claims are the shadow figures seen wandering about the cemetery. People have reported seeing them rise from behind crumbling tombstones, as well as emerging from the woods, to walk the perimeter of the grounds. Fast-moving shadows have approached some visitors, who then felt cold spots rush through them. Sometimes, investigators hear wails and screams before the arrival and after the passing of the shadows. Others have reported hearing these chilling cries coming from deep within the woods, even when the dark figures have not shown themselves.

There are a few other creepy accounts from the Gates of Hell. One is about a tombstone near the center of the cemetery that will glow with an unexplained light. No one knows what causes this glow. Is this where the alleged gate opens? Another involves the ghosts of children who go home with those who see them. One in particular—that of a little girl in a white dress—supposedly went home with a child and visited him several times in a span of a few weeks. Trees supposedly move around the cemetery. This account is quite odd and we're not sure of its origin. Could it simply be that the wind was blowing them around, or were they supposed to be actually moving?

A psychic medium did claim to have made contact with the spirit of a young man who hanged himself from a tree there sometime back in the 1980s. Maybe this has something to do with the moving tree.

Others have heard whispering voices warning them to leave the graveyard right away. Others have felt strangled by something unseen, while hearing disembodied wicked laughter. One man said something scratched him so badly that his arm bled heavily before an invisible force pulled him to the ground.

There is a legend that there was once, or still is, a former witch's cabin near the woods. If this is the case, that could explain the rumors of rituals and the screams from the darkness. It would also provide a possible lead to the origins of the Gates of Hell legend. It has also been said there is a lone grave located somewhere beyond the cemetery. Could this be the resting place of the alleged witch, or is it just complete rubbish? There has been a woman in white witnessed there, staring at people walking through the woods. Who she is, no one knows.

If even a portion of these accounts have truth to them, then it's not hard to see why some have elected to call Grandview Cemetery the Gates of Hell. With legends of witches and Satanism abound, it is not surprising some have claimed there is a passage to the dark world somewhere inside. With that many claims, it's hard to shrug it off and think nothing has gone on there. But, could it be just a rash of urban legends run amuck? Guess there's really only one way to find out.

ST. MARTIN'S SKELETONS

JACOB FLOYD AND JENNY FLOYD

Though it's not a cemetery, St. Martin's of Tours Catholic Church on Shelby Street in Downtown Louisville does have some remains resting within their establishment. The church itself is one of many churches established in the mid-1800s (1853 for this church) by German immigrants on the east side of the city. Expansion on the church took place in the 1860s with renovations performed in the 1890s. Today, it is one of the oldest larger structures standing in Louisville, and one of the antebellum buildings open to the public in the city.

The historic aspects aren't the only singular qualities about St. Martin's. In 1901, the Cistercian Nuns of Agnani, Italy had to relinquish their sanctuary, and in doing so, their relics needed storing elsewhere. Among those sent to St. Martin's of Tours, were the enshrined skeletons of two martyrs: St. Magnus and St. Bonosa.

According to some reports, the identity of St. Magnus is Magnus of Trani, the Apulian bishop. No confirmation of this claim exists. St. Bonosa is a Roman virgin. The martyrs died in either 3 or 4AD. Allegedly, Bonosa execution came due to her faith in Christianity. Different stories exist regarding Magnus's execution. Some say Bonosa's execution in the Colosseum moved him to convert to Christianity, which eventually resulted in his execution. Another story claims Magnus stepped into the arena to save Bonosa, which led to his instant demise. The Catholic Church makes no claims to know if either of these stories is true. The skeletal remains of the martyrs lie in glass reliquaries beneath the altars on each side of the pulpit at the front of the church.

A University of Louisville archeologist by the name of Phillip DiBlasi studied the remains of both martyrs in 2012.

He found that Bonosa was a Caucasian woman, aged about twenty-four. Magnus's DNA testing was not as complete, but what results could be found deduced he died in his forties and was of part European and part African descent. The full story and identity of these martyrs will likely remain a mystery. Nonetheless, their presence at St. Martin's of Tours makes for a unique visitation.

There are no hauntings to speak of at St. Martin's of Tours. We felt that the fact they have centuries-old skeletons enshrined there in the church, open for public viewing at all hours of the day, is haunting enough. Nonetheless, the church itself, beyond even the fascinating remains, is worth a visit. It is quite exquisite in its design and décor, and a piece of city history.

JACOB FLOYD AND JENNY FLOYD

THERE'S A PLOT IN THE LOT

Louisville's Strange and Unusual Haunts

KENTUCKY'S HAUNTED GRAVEYARDS

An interesting place stands near the Rafferty's parking lot off Breckinridge Lane in Louisville, Kentucky. At the lot's edge, encompassed by tall bushes, is the Burke Family Plot. People have dubbed this small cemetery, erected circa mid-1800s, the "Cemetery That Isn't" because it isn't even visible to anyone driving through the lot.

Maybe in the winter, when the bushes are more skeletal, someone might see the pointed tops of one of the tall monuments; or, if someone just happens to be looking at the right time, they'll see the small space between bushes where the gate lies, and the white of one of the large stones glares back at them. It's not impossible to see, but it is hard to notice. One could park right next to it and never know the graveyard is there.

Although there have never been any reported ghosts or spooky goings-on, we have had some pretty interesting moments, and even one intense spirit box session there.

When you pass the gate that stands between the bushes, you find just a small plot of land with thick, rich grass, four adult gravesites, and one infant sealed off from the world by a cracked concrete wall. One site is without its monument, knocked over and left lying in the swarming grass. Someone informed us the area used to be a horse farm, and if this were true, we would deduce the land belonged to the Burke Family.

At different times, we have heard different things said to us on the spirit box. A voice came through once, telling Jacob to quit standing on someone's grave. He was unaware he was doing so, and when he looked down, he saw there was some concrete in the grass beneath his feet. Another voice told us to get out and shut up, and even had some unfriendly swears thrown our way. But, we also had an apology from a lady's voice come out to us afterward. But, after a while, we began to think these remarks were not for us, but for someone else coming through on the spirit box, like we were intruding upon an otherworldly conversation.

We've never caught anything interesting on any pictures we've taken in the small cemetery, beyond strange orbs floating around the graves. As far as orbs are concerned, we believe there is something to them sometimes, depending on the type of orb one catches, but we also believe there is a rational explanation in most cases, most of which are pollen, dust, or bugs creating the orbs. But, when thick, bright orbs with visible energy inside shows up, especially in a place where we have had questionable responses on our box, it is something we feel is worth considering.

But, haunted or not, if you're ever in the area, taking a trip to the Kaden Towers or Books-a-Million, we recommend at least a quick peek at this secluded little gemstone of history hidden in the middle of a bustling chain of shopping centers and restaurants. Just look for the tall, fat bushes standing sentinel.

THE LONELY GHOST
OF SARAH MITCHELL

JACOB FLOYD AND JENNY FLOYD

Located upon Mitchell Hill Road in Fairdale, KY lies a small graveyard by the side of the road known as Mitchell Cemetery. The cemetery is right at the top of the hill where teenagers and young adults would gather to drag race down a steep, winding road. Races through this area, known to locals at Hot-Rod Haven, resulted in the death of more than twenty-five people between the 1940s and 1970s. Most believe these deaths came from crashes caused by the twisty nature of the road, and the sharp left turn at the end. There are others, however, who insist a curse lies upon this dangerous road.

The curse, they say, began on September 23rd, 1946, as a young couple—Roy Clark and Sarah Mitchell—was on their way to their high school prom. As Roy navigated the car to the bottom and into the sharp left turn, he somehow lost control. The vehicle crashed, killing him and Sarah. No one really knows why Roy lost control. He did not have a wild reputation, and it is unlikely he drove recklessly. Due to this, some believe in the curse, as many other fatal automobile accidents occurred there. However, many chalk these tragedies up to the reckless racing conducted by the youth whose vehicles used to roar down the road for bragging rights.

Ever since Roy and Sarah's deaths, rumors of a girl's ghost haunting Mitchell Cemetery have become part of the Hot Rod Haven legend. Many believe this to be Sarah's spirit searching for her lost love, as her grave lies there in her family cemetery. Reports say she wanders the grounds, dressed in a white dress, sometimes glowing in the night, with an air of sadness and distress. Others claim to have seen her simply hovering near her grave, looking forlorn and somber. If this specter does exist, Sarah Mitchell is the most likely source for its energy.

KENTUCKY'S HAUNTED GRAVEYARDS

The lonely ghost of Sarah Mitchell isn't the only eerie tale told about Hot Rod Haven. When we were younger, there used to be a story about a car with one headlight helmed by a maniacal driver chasing people travelling down Mitchell Hill Road after dark. As the story goes, during a race, the driver found himself caught behind another vehicle, slowing him down. The driver pulled the car as close to the vehicle in front of him as he could get to force the other driver to speed up. When the driver did not increase the car's speed, the racer slung his one-headlight vehicle to the side to pass the car before him, sped off to catch his opponent in the race, but crashed before reaching the end.

Now, the story says, if someone is driving too slowly down Mitchell Road at nighttime, they'll see the one headlight of the phantom car appear behind them in the distance. The car will speed up, drawing the light nearer, until it is right behind the person's vehicle. In the light of the vehicle, one will see a slight fog enveloping the front end. After riding behind them for a while, the car will wildly speed past them and vanish into the darkness.

We're not sure if the origin story to this alleged haunt holds any truth. There also isn't any information of the story online. Whether it is an old legend, or one made up by high school kids a few decades back, we don't know. We *do* know teens in our area told the story at least in the nineties and early 2000s. However, Jacob *did* have a strange experience one night on Mitchell Hill Road while riding with some friends.

Sometime in 1998, maybe early 1999, Jacob was riding with two of his friends on Mitchell Hill Road. His friend Ronnie was driving and his friend John sat in the passenger seat. Jacob sat stretched out in the backseat. While travelling down the road, they were talking about the legend. A few minutes later, Ronnie called the others' attention to a light in the distance behind the car.

After turning to look through the rear window, Jacob said, "It looks like a car with one headlight," and then he chuckled. They all had a laugh about that, but a few seconds later, the light began to approach quickly, erratically, as if the car were swerving about the road. He then said, "Man, they're driving crazy."

A few seconds later, the car was right on their rear end, moving back and forth. Jacob watched as the one headlight nearly disappeared behind his friend's car, as the vehicle following them had moved in so close. "He's right on your ass, man," he told Ronnie.

John insisted Ronnie speed up. Jacob told him not to, because he wanted to see if the car would speed past them and vanish in the darkness. Sure enough, maybe a minute later, the car yanked out from behind them and sped around the car, then blasted off into the night. They all watched as the red taillights began to fade.

"Speed up, Ronnie!" Jacob said. "Follow him."

Ronnie accelerated to see if he could catch a glimpse at what might have been the phantom vehicle. Jacob can't recall exactly what Ronnie was driving, but it wasn't a fast car. He and one of his friends used to call it the Squeakster because it whined if it went too fast. So, by the time he had rounded a curve and hit a straightaway, the taillights were no longer visible. They never saw the car by the time they reached the end of the road.

This, of course, doesn't mean Jacob and his friends encountered the phantom car of legend. It simply could have been an impatient driver in a hurry, some other kids acting silly, or someone driving while under the influence. However, even though Ronnie's car was not fast, the vehicle that passed them would have had to drive at an incredibly high speed to be gone from sight by the time they reached the bottom. Was it the one-eyed spirit of a crashed automobile, driven by someone determined to win the race at all costs? We'll never know, but it was an interesting experience.

THE HAUNTING OF OCTAVIA HATCHER

Kentucky's Strange and Unusual Haunts

The story of Octavia Hatcher is one of legend around Pikeville. Articles and shows have documented both her tragic death and alleged haunting. As with many urban legends, the truth gets marred with each retelling. Octavia's death and the details surrounding it changed often, and they have created quite a sensational campfire tale. But, despite all the grisly accounts that blur the line between fact and fiction, the real story is both tragic and poignant.

The tale begins in Pike County, famous sight of the legendary feud between the Hatfield and McCoys. In the 1880s, an eighteen-year-old James Hatcher started a warehouse business and worked to become one of the wealthiest men in the state. His fortune was substantial by the age of thirty. He met Octavia Smith, daughter of a well-to-do dry goods merchant, Jacob Smith, and his wife, Pricey. Hatcher and Smith wed in 1889, and on January 4th, 1891, had their only son, Jacob, named after Octavia's father. The child was born ill and died in a few hours. Octavia fell into a deep depression.

Octavia became seriously ill soon after young Jacob's death. She was bedridden in April and then slipped into a coma. Upon medical examination, doctors pronounced her dead on May 2nd, 1891, having passed from an unknown illness. Her husband had her interred at Pikeville Cemetery next to her son. In 1892, James Hatcher erected a monument in her honor, with her holding her beloved Jacob in her arms.

This is where the story gets questionable. Since the summer was so hot, James Hatcher had both the funeral and burial rushed so Octavia's body would not spoil. Due to the rushed nature of the services, the embalmer did not embalm Octavia's body, resulting in her living burial.

Not long after, others in town developed this inexplicable sleeping sickness and began to slip into comas, as well. Allegedly, doctors determined the bite of the tsetse fly—indigenous to Africa—that caused this disease. Once James Hatcher caught wind of this, he rushed to have the body of his late wife exhumed. When her grave was unearthed and the coffin opened, a grisly scene awaited them. They found the interior lining torn apart with claw marks, and fingernails dug into the wood. There were scratchers torn across Octavia's face, frozen in a scream. Her hands rested in claw-like positions, as if she had been desperately trying to dig her way out.

The discovery crushed James. Already heartbroken by what he believed to be the sudden death of his beloved, to find that she met such a disturbing end made matters far worse. He then had her reburied.

As we said before, the legend evolves, dramatically sensationalizing Octavia's death, some believe. There is no documentation of Octavia's premature burial. Some who debunk this story claim that if such a terrifying incident occurred in a town as small as Pikeville, there would undoubtedly be a record of the event. Yet, no one who claims this took place has been able to cite any sources for this information. Also, there would almost certainly be record of her exhumation, yet there is none, apparently. That is, of course, unless James Hatcher, being such a wealthy and prominent man in town, had these records erased so none would discover what a horrible fate befell poor Octavia.

With that said, there is also no record of the sleeping sickness, and it has been argued that the theory of the tsetse fly bite is unlikely due to its African origin and the likelihood that if such a fly had found its way over here it would have only affected a few people. Other claims that some sort of gas from the coalmines could have caused the sleeping sickness, but this is mere theory without any evidence to support it.

On top of this, there have been other versions of this story told through the years. One of those alterations being that Octavia died while still pregnant, which is almost certainly untrue. But, storytellers also go on to say the mourners present at Octavia's funeral could actually hear the baby crying inside the coffin. Jacob's headstone is by Octavia's grave, and it indicates that he definitely preceded her in death, so there is practically no way this is true.

To help quell the spreading of false tales, a monument explaining Octavia's true demise stands near the grave. Also, since some unprincipled riffraff have broken the statue of the baby from Octavia's arms, a fence surrounds the monument to discourage other rabble from vandalizing it. Also, the folks who live near there keep an eye on the area so no one else does something as reprehensible as this. How sad it is that there are people who would commit such an egregious act.

Locals tell stories of Octavia's ghost hanging around the grave. The month of May is the best time for sightings. Those who live on the hill near the graveyard have claimed to hear a woman weeping near Octavia's grave late in the night when no one is present. Some have even said the sound of a baby crying has accompanied the weeping. People have seen mysterious blue lights floating around the grave, as well as swirling mist hovering at the foot of Octavia's statue. Others who have stood at her marker have been overwhelmed with the sudden onset of intense sadness or immense dread. A woman in black kneels at Jacob's grave and weeps. People claim the statue will sometimes turn its back on the town for the disrespect of her grave. Though the turning of the statue is likely a college prank.

Those who try to debunk the story of Octavia's ghost have cited a tragic ghost story much older than Octavia's. There is a story about a woman holding a baby was walking along a road near Ivy Creek late at night, and a large boulder fell from the hillside and landed upon her and the child, killing both. Allegedly, they remained buried beneath that rock and, sometimes, at night, the woman, all in black, walks around the stone in search of her baby. On the anniversary of their death, her dying wails echo through the darkness. Some believe this story to be the true origin of the story applied to Octavia Hatcher, and that's from where her legend comes. Even the part about the statue of Octavia holding the baby may have derived from this tale, since some claim the statue never actually held the baby, and she actually held a parasol with an immense ring on it in her right hand.

JACOB FLOYD AND JENNY FLOYD

THE SOULS STILL SHINE
AT MY OLD KENTUCKY HOME

Kentucky's Haunted Mansions

If you ever went to elementary school in the state of Kentucky, you have heard the old folk classic, "My Old Kentucky Home." The year credited to the song's creation is 1852. In 1928, Kentucky adopted the ballad as the state's official song. It is a mandatory melody learned by young students in music class all across the state. A staple of Kentucky tradition, balladeer and composer, Stephen Foster, was inspired to pen the legendary Bluegrass anthem after visiting Federal Hill Mansion, located on My Old Kentucky Home State Park.

My Old Kentucky Home, originally known as Federal Hill, spreads symbolic of a time of progression, like a spiritual photograph that has eternally captured the essence of the days when the nation was about to move forward. Though it was always a grand estate full of beauty and elegance, it now represents a tradition of change, still with southern praxis, and a legacy of loyalty that pumps through the very heart of the state. Kentuckians come from all around, with a sense of pride, to visit one of the most significant historical landmarks in the entire commonwealth.

But, Federal Hill did not begin as such a monumental site. Its beginning was relatively humble, and it's history intricate. There are a few names associated with the evolution of the park's legacy. While most sites of this magnitude often owe their fame primarily to one remarkable person, Federal Hill's advancement was, historically, a joint effort. But, there is always a beginning to every legend, and Federal Hill's most noteworthy source of origin can be pinned to a man by the name of John Rowan.

JOHN ROWAN

JACOB FLOYD AND JENNY FLOYD

John Rowan was born on July 12th, 1773 to William Rowan, a captain during the Revolutionary War, and Sarah Elizabeth Cooper Rowan, who journeyed by boat with their children from Pennsylvania to Kentucky County, Virginia where they had previously purchased land. After the war efforts depleted their resources, their hope was to make good on all the farming and business opportunities available in the area.

What was to be a seven-day trip down the Monongahela and Ohio Rivers turned into six months thanks to the harsh winter. The Rowans arrived in Louisville and spent another month going west to settle Fort Vienna, where they spent six years. At the time, Bardstown schools provided excellent education, so the Rowans moved there to give their children better opportunities. Once there, they moved into a log cabin owned by John Lytle.

John Rowan studied law under a preeminent lawyer named George Nichols, who was a friend of Thomas Jefferson. Once his studies were complete, he returned home and married Ann Lytle, John Lytle's daughter, in 1794. Ann's father then gifted the land the Rowans once lived on to the newlywed couple, and gave them a trust fund with more than enough money to improve the log cabin that sat upon it.

In 1795, the Rowans made their first improvement on Federal Hill: a modest one-story brick building that is now the rear wing of the mansion. But, over the years, their family increased with the addition of nine children and the current house was simply not large enough.

Thanks not only to the trust fund, but also to success gained through various business transactions, farming profits, and John's personal career, the Rowans could afford to make more additions to their home. Due to the cost of importing the materials, however, the construction would be gradual, and it wasn't until 1818 that Federal Hill Mansion was complete. In 1812, while the home was under construction, a fire broke out and destroyed the log cabin they had lived in, so they had to move into the section of the mansion that was completed.

Today, Federal Hill is a three-story Federal style home, with the top floor being significantly smaller in area than the other two. The home sits on a limestone foundation, built with bricks fired on-site. The Federal style was popular style in America in the 19th century. It is a very symmetrical design utilizing extremely smooth exteriors and geometrical shapes. The design came from ancient Roman architecture, adopted in an attempt by the United States to associate itself with the well-known democracies of the past. The etymology of the name comes from the political movement of the Federal Party that was popular at the time. Patriotism bleeds through Federal Hill, not just in the architectural style, but also in the symbolism of the number thirteen used throughout the home: thirteen original rooms, thirteen steps on each stairway, walls that are thirteen inches thick, and thirteen windows across the front of the house, all to represent the original thirteen colonies.

Builders used mostly resources found on the farm to construct the interior frame of the home, and had materials imported from the eastern United States for everything else. The Rowans always maintained style. All of the furnishing was costly and of the highest fashion. John Rowan made sure that his family enjoyed his successes. But, despite the comfort he earned for him and his loved ones, Rowan's days were not without scandal.

In 1801, John Rowan was involved in a very controversial legal matter with a man by the name of Dr. James Chambers. While playing cards with Dr. Chambers and three other men at Duncan McLean's Tavern in Bardstown, Rowan had too many drinks and agreed to play for money. While engaged in Vingt-et-un—or, Black Jack—an argument began between Chambers and Rowan. Some say the men were tossing insults back and forth, and others say the spat was over who was more fluent in either Latin or Greek. Whatever it was, it evolved into a minor scuffle.

Eventually, it led to a duel. The details of how it escalated into such a severe matter are sketchy. One story states Chambers immediately issued the challenge, only for Rowan to refuse it. Another claim is that Chambers issued the challenge by mail. Both men's seconds met on February 1st to discuss the rules of engagement. Rowan wanted the matter dropped, but Chambers would not retract the challenge. The duel took place near Bardstown two days later. Both men missed their first shots, but Rowan's second shot hit Chambers in the chest. Rowan had the seriously wounded Chambers placed in his own carriage and taken in for medical attention. While doctors tended to him, Chambers said he did not want Rowan prosecuted for the shooting. Chambers died the next day.

Despite Chambers' insistence Rowan not face any legal action related to the duel, a posse of Chambers' friends rode to Rowan's house to punish him, but Rowan dressed one of his slaves in his own coat and hat and then sent him from the house on horseback as a diversion. The lynch mob pursued the slave, but he got away, sparing Rowan.

This was not the end of the backlash. The man who owned the land upon which the duel transpired swore out a warrant for murder against Rowan. But, the presiding judge declared that there was not enough evidence to indict Rowan.

Rowan had a very active and successful political career. He served as a US Senator from 1825 to 1831, was a member of the House of Representatives from 1807 to 1809, and was the third Secretary of State from 1803 to 1807. He also served a number of terms in the Kentucky House of Representatives. Throughout his years, he was instrumental in the legal education of many men, and in the advancement of numerous political careers. He eulogized his good friend George Rogers Clark in 1818. Later, he became chummy with Andrew Jackson and the two often visited one another once Jackson's presidential term was complete.

Tragedy struck the Rowan family in 1833 during the cholera epidemic: three of the nine children fell victim to the ailment's fatal sting. Their son, William, passed away, as did his wife. Their daughter, Mary Jane, died alongside her husband and daughter, and their other son, Atkinson, perished as well. Rowan lost his sister, Elizabeth, and her husband, too.

Adding to his prominence in 1836, John Rowan and two other men started the Louisville Medical Institute, which later became the University of Louisville Medical School, and served as the inaugural president until 1842. He was also president of the Kentucky Historical Society from 1838 until his death in 1843.

John Rowan lies at the family burial ground on Federal Hill. Since his parents had no grave markers of their own, he insisted in his will that his grave have no marker, as well. Despite his wishes, the family placed a sizeable marker over his grave some years later.

JOHN JR., REBECCA CARNES, AND STEPHEN FOSTER

John Rowan's only remaining son, his namesake John Jr., married Rebecca Carnes in 1835 and abandoned his law practice to settle a farm with her near Vicksburg, MS. But, the climate there affected Rebecca's health, so they gave up the farm and returned to Federal Hill.

John Jr. found much difficulty in selecting a career, but eventually settled into public office. Being aficionados of the arts, they made sure to keep Federal Hill an ideal place for many young writers and authors to highlight their talents. Among the artists who visited was their cousin, famed singer-songwriter, Stephen Foster. Influenced by the beatific nature of Federal Hill and the sprawling Kentucky landscape, as well as the Harriet Beecher Stowe novel, *Uncle Tom's Cabin*, Foster composed an anti-slavery song he called, "Poor Uncle Tom, Goodnight," with the intention of speaking out against the inhuman nature of such an institution. But, the detailed depiction of southern Kentucky lifestyle and scenery warranted a change in the title, and the song became, "My Old Kentucky Home." As the years progressed and popularity of the song grew, many people came to associate it with the mansion and began coming from all over to see the song's inspiration.

Debts for the Rowans piled up, as the farm income was not enough to pay the bills. The struggle became more daunting as the family unit expanded to ten children. Then, on August 14th, 1855, John Jr. was tending to his sick daughter, Margaret (known in her life primarily as Madge), in her upstairs bedroom, and fell asleep sitting on a windowsill. Rebecca later called up to John, shaking him from his slumber, which caused him to fall from the window and plummet to his death. This tragedy left Rebecca a widow with mounting debts and now barely any income with which to pay them. She was in dire straits and unequipped to manage the estate's affairs while juggling the responsibilities of running the family.

MADGE AND MY OLD KENTUCKY HOME

Though it was a struggle, Rebecca managed to keep the unit afloat. When she died in 1897, the estate of John Rowan, Sr. remained unsettled. With the estate split between his heirs, John Jr. and Rebecca's daughter, Madge, each received half of Federal Hill's mansion and farm.

Madge was the last woman to live in the mansion. The townspeople thought well of her. She was considered sophisticated and charming, and a perfect portrait of the ideal southern dame. She was often a gracious and affable hostess, always willing to tell some tales about the Rowan Family's decorated past.

During this time, "My Old Kentucky Home" kept gaining fame. People were still pouring into Bardstown to visit Federal Hill. On March 20, 1920, the state of Kentucky decided to enshrine Federal Hill due to its historic significance as a symbol of American hospitality. Madge eventually sold the house and the land for $65,000 to the state, who performed restorations on the home. On July 4th, 1923, Federal Hill officially became My Old Kentucky Home with more than 15,000 spectators present to celebrate the iconic mansion's preservation.

Since then, the land and manor have undergone many renovations. There have also been numerous attractions and events held there through the years to celebrate the history as well as the impact Federal Hill's timeline has had on southern America.

The ties of the Rowan family bloodline are like spiritual veins pumping energy through the walls of My Old Kentucky Home. Such historic significance exists there, attributed to that one family. The state's objective is to preserve the estate and the memory of the family who built it. In this bustling age of technology and microwave societies, many people don't want to slow down long enough to hear about culture. So, even if time erases the Rowan Family from the minds of the locals, their lasting spirit will try to hang on to let visitors know they are still present; and, it seems they have had some success in making their presence felt, because there have been several claims of paranormal activity experienced at one of Kentucky's most famous locations.

The large obelisk marker placed to distinguish the grave of John Sr. seems to be a source of ghostly contention in the Federal Hill Cemetery. Reports say that the stone fell over not long after its placement; and, when it soon fell over again after someone reset it. Ever since then, this process has been ongoing. Someone will find the marker dumped over, put it back up, only to find it down again later. People have seen the image of the Rowan family patriarch leaning against the marker with a contemptuous look upon his face, trying to push it over.

A former groundskeeper at the estate once spotted a figure in the cemetery messing around by the marker. He described the intruder as seeming very agitated, striking at the stone, and flinging himself against it. The man's movements were somewhat erratic and they made the groundskeeper nervous. But, he thought he finally caught one of the vandals who like to invade the family plot and knock the stone over. So, he called to the figure. The man kept pushing at the stone, seeming to grip the stone with his hands and move himself back and forth as if he was attempting to pull the headstone out of place. The form knelt down and started hitting the base of the stone, and looking as if he were digging in the dirt. As the groundskeeper opened the gate, the figure went behind the stone and did not come back out. The groundskeeper checked behind the stone and found no one. He stood in the middle of the plot and surveyed the grounds but never saw anyone running away. He said he couldn't make out any details about the man he saw, but he wonders if maybe he really did see the ghost of John Sr. trying to take down the offending tombstone placed on his grave against his wishes, or just some slippery hooligan who snuck in to do damage to the gravestone.

The sound of banjo music plays through the house, from hallways and empty rooms. The tunes range from sad dirges to upbeat folk music. Some have even reported hearing a man's voice singing indecipherable lyrics.

A woman who was once cleaning on the second floor walked into one of the old bedrooms and saw a man dressed in "old time clothes" sitting on the windowsill. Startled, she asked the man what he was doing up there in the house because no visitors were supposed to be there, yet. The man didn't answer her. He didn't even look at her. When she looked closer at him, she discovered she could see right through him and he looked to be sleeping. After a few seconds, she recalled that the man looked strikingly like the pictures she had seen of one of the men around the house. After his image faded from her sight, she told someone else about the incident. She then heard the story about how John Jr. fell to his death from a window upstairs, and when shown his picture, she identified the man as the same one she saw upstairs.

Doors open and close on their own, which many say is the ghost of Rebecca Carnes. Through the years, people have reported seeing a woman walking the halls with a candle, even in the day, checking the doors diligently. They say the woman looks like Rebecca Carnes.

There have been a few incidents where an older man in a Revolutionary War uniform walked through the family cemetery. Though no one knows who this is, most believe it to be the spirit of William Rowan—the man who brought the Rowans to Federal Hill. Maybe he is searching for his unmarked grave, or perhaps he is just taking his turn watching the graveyard. We think he might be waiting to tell his son to stop the foolishness with the tombstone because it is not an important matter.

It seems as though the Rowan family holds a stern vigil over Federal Hill. They aren't riotous or bothersome spirits; they simply wander about the home and land. Whether we decide to call the place Federal Hill or My Old Kentucky

Home, it's always going to be the Rowan family home to them, and they're probably not going to leave it until they're ready.

JACOB FLOYD AND JENNY FLOYD

THE GLOWING TOMBSTONE
Kentucky's Strange and Unusual Haunts

Gibson Cemetery in Benton holds a particular tombstone of legend – one that often glows a mysterious green light. The legend of the Glowing Tombstone has led to Gibson Cemetery's nickname, the Glowing Tombstone Cemetery. Many people say they've seen it glowing both day and night. No one knows what exactly makes it glow, but there is a legend told explaining the illumination.

Long ago, an old married couple lived by Gibson Cemetery, and had lived there for many years. One night, they heard commotion outside. The husband went to check it out and could hear that it was coming from their barn out back. With rumors of cult activity taking place in the area, they feared someone was performing some bizarre rite or ritual on their property. The old man was ready to run these hooligans off, so he crossed the backyard and entered the barn.

A long time passed as the old woman waited in the house for her husband to return. After a while, she decided to go check on him. She too then exited the house and ventured to the barn. But when she stepped into the barn, a ghastly sight greeted her. Her husband hung dead from one of the rafters, a rope tied tightly around his neck. Signs of a struggle were all around her, and she then knew the rumors of the cult to be true.

She laid her husband to rest in Gibson Cemetery. Now people say his angry spirit remains in that barn, awaiting vengeance. When the old man's restless soul has its ire up, his tombstone begins to glow. Some say his soul senses bad energy near, and believes it to be his killers. The glow is to let his killers know that his body might be in the ground, but is soul awaits their return to the barn so he can gain retribution.

The house the couple once lived in is no longer there. Either it fell down or someone tore it down long ago. Allegedly, another couple attempted to build another house there but it collapsed each time and they never could finish the project. Perhaps the old man's powerful, angry energy kept knocking it down.

Whether or not this tombstone actually glows, we don't know. We have not seen it for ourselves. If it does, it very well could be foxfire, which grows in many places throughout Kentucky. Foxfire is a bioluminescent fungus that glows green. It can be found in Kentucky woods and caves, and there's no reason to think it might not be on this tombstone from time to time.

Unless it really is the old man's raging spirit seething for revenge.

JACOB FLOYD AND JENNY FLOYD

THE HAUNTED MAUSOLEUM

KENTUCKY'S HAUNTED GRAVEYARDS

Evergreen Funeral Home and Cemetery is located on a busy stretch of Preston Highway across from the Louisville International Airport in Louisville's Newburg neighborhood. They offer both funeral services and burial. The land consists of long fields of gravesites, exterior mausoleums at the front, and new mausoleums in the back. A number of columbaria with mausoleums stand around the large lake at the front of the cemetery, where many waterfowl live and drink.

The establishment of Evergreen Cemetery took place in 1912, and had its first interment in 1914. The funeral home didn't exist until 1992. Later that year, Jacob's father had his funeral there, after suddenly dying of a massive heart attack at the age of forty. Evergreen is the burial site for many members on both sides of Jacob's family. Jenny too has many family members interred there. We have visited there many times over the years since we've been together. At first, we visited only for family members laid to rest. When we started conducting paranormal investigations and cemetery photography, we came to Evergreen for those purposes as well.

The land is quiet the further back you go from the bustling highway. In the back, there is almost complete silence, except for the planes flying over and the noises from the nearby Male High School. During our times taking photographs and running the spirit box around there, Jenny always wanted to avoid the first mausoleum in the front center, where out front sits a large family plot. Something about the building always made her uneasy. It wasn't until we finally decided to check the building out that we figured out why.

When we entered, we could smell something foul. We don't want to say it was death, but there was a hint of decay mixed with the smell of bleach. On the floor was a large grate, and beyond that was the area where services take place. Leaves scattered along the interior floor. There was a creepy feeling inside, though Jacob attributed that to the quietness and emptiness. From one end to the other, the building was not very long. There were places for bodies along the walls, and in small rooms at each end, barred by a small gate. The gates at both ends were open.

We went into the small room at the north end of the building. Jenny turned on the spirit box and began talking. There were no responses on the box. When she turned it off, they heard a series of bumps from the center of the mausoleum. Fearing that someone had wandered in, Jacob stepped out first to ensure there was no one else. When he saw there was not, Jenny came out too, and they closed the gate to the room.

We then decided to check the area to see if there was an animal or perhaps a person in the small room at the south end. The interior leaves very little room for someone to hide, and had anyone been in there, we would have seen them. By the time we reached the other room, no one was present. So, we went into that room and Jenny turned on the spirit box again.

After asking a few more questions and receiving no responses, she turned off the box. This time, we heard soft voices speaking. Voices echo in the mausoleum, yet these did not. We listened for a moment, trying to understand what they were saying, never able to decipher the words. After a minute or so, the talking ceased. We waited to hear the front door open and close, but it did not. What we did hear was a loud scraping sound, followed by a loud thud. Jacob stepped out again and saw no one. Though both of us were sure that was not the door to the building, Jacob quickly went to check just in case. No one was there and no one was near the building outside.

Jenny came out again. We walked the floor once more to see if we saw anyone. When we reached the room at the north end, we both stopped and stared at the open gate. Jacob had closed it on the way out a few minutes prior. Someone—or something—had pushed it back open. Someone—or something—had just been in there with us!

We walked outside and looked around, thinking we might see someone hurrying off. There was no one: we saw no one walking away, no one standing nearby, nor any cars driving down the paths. We were alone in the cemetery, as it would seem—at least, in the area around the mausoleum.

During one of our signings, we told someone of this incident. They said they too heard tales of that mausoleum being haunted, and of people having weird feelings in and around the building. They agreed the building had an eerie aura, and that the entire graveyard was spooky.

Jacob once visited the niche that held his father's urn in one of the buildings close to the entrance. We had the spirit box running and we were asking questions. Some answers came back that sounded something like his father's voice. Jacob attempted some questions. The answers were hard to decipher, but the same voice responded each time. Once, Jacob informed the voice of something that happened in his life, and the voice responded, "Oh yeah?"

We don't know much about the history of Evergreen, save for common knowledge. We don't know if anything bad transpired there, or if the land has some dark history. We do know it stands on wetlands, and many of the tombstones tilt, lean over, and begin to fall. Maybe that causes some unrest among the spirits. Towards the front, off to the right as you enter, employees informally refer to that nearby section as "Babyland," where lie those who died as infants. The death of a child is always a sad affair, and perhaps that brings some paranormal energy to the land.

THE MAPLEWOOD MONUMENTS

JACOB FLOYD AND JENNY FLOYD

Maplewood Cemetery in the far southeast town of Mayfield, Kentucky isn't exactly haunted, but it contains something rather haunting. While there are no ghosts lurking about the grounds, towards the center of the cemetery stands a very sinister vision. Eighteen large statues stand eerily still, gazing to the east over the field of the dead. This unsettling collection of stone monuments bears the name of their creator—the Wooldridge Monuments.

In 1892, after the last of his sisters passed away, Col. Henry G. Wooldridge commissioned these statues to commemorate those in life who mattered most to him. Wooldridge bought a lot of land in Maplewood Cemetery for himself as well as the monuments. He was a lifelong bachelor, so he had no children, and so had only his blood relations and a few animals to call family. The erection of these statues would last from 1892 until his own death on May 30th, 1899.

Dubbed the Strange Procession that Never Moves, these monuments vary in size, and include the likenesses of Wooldridge himself, a monument of Wooldridge upon his horse Fop, his mother Keziah; his brothers Alfred, John, Josiah, and W.H.; his sisters Minerva, Narcissa, and Susan; his nieces Maude and Minnie, as well as a fox and a deer with Wooldridge's two dogs—Bob and Towhead—in pursuit. There is another story about Minnie, which claims she was the colonel's childhood sweetheart who passed away in a horse-riding accident, and this led to him remaining a bachelor. Though each of these family members has a memorial, Col. Wooldridge is the only one buried at Maplewood.

Despite there being no ghost stories tied to this unmoving procession, many who visit Maplewood find it a sight both fascinating and ominous.

JACOB FLOYD AND JENNY FLOYD

THE AIRPORT GRAVESITE

KENTUCKY'S HAUNTED GRAVEYARDS

Louisville is home to the world's largest package-handling facility—the UPS Worldport—which is also the global air hub for the United Parcel Service. With more than 150 miles of conveyor belts and 5.2 million square foot facility, the Worldport serves as the central sorting location for UPS, handling millions of packages daily. This compound is responsible for more than two hundred companies relocating to Kentucky, creating more than 62,000 jobs. UPS's presence in the state is crucial to the expansion of the state's commerce.

While just about everyone knows of UPS, and most in the state know its significance to the state's economy, there is a little secret many people don't know about the Worldport. That secret is the gravesite preserved at the heart of the facility.

Surrounded by the logistics facility and the many airport runaways is a small patch of grass with a fence around it, the Kentucky Air National Guard uncovered the remains in 1972. Archaeologists from the University of Louisville then investigated the site, determining the nature of the remains. UPS leaves the land undisturbed due to the Kentucky Antiquities Act, which prevents such sites from desecration. Since the discovery of this Native American burial ground predated the existence of the Worldport, UPOS built the hub around the site, which is now preserved.

Though people have said there is paranormal activity around the burial ground, no one has even produced specifics, leaving us to believe that these are just rumors with not reports to corroborate them.

JACOB FLOYD AND JENNY FLOYD

A HORSE IN A HAUNT
Kentucky's Strange and Unusual Haunts

Located in Calloway County, towards the far southwestern edge of the state, about twelve miles from Murray, is the haunted Asbury Cemetery. Large oaks and evergreens surround the cemetery. Without counting the unmarked graves, there are about four hundred people interred at Asbury, making it small by today's standards. Not so small, perhaps, by the standards of its own day, being located in such a rural area.

The oldest grave dates back to 1824, and is for a toddler who was not even two years old. That's an old stone for Calloway County considering its founding came in 1822. But there are plenty of graves for people who were born in the 1700s, including one who was born before the Colonies were free – a man by the name of Kimbrough T. Ogilvie. Ogilvie was born in 1763 and fought in the Guilford County Regiment for the North Carolina Revolution Militia during the American Revolution. This regiment was active from 1775-1783, and we couldn't find specific dates when Ogilvie participated, but that would put him in the war anytime between the ages of eleven and twenty, and we believe closer to the latter is more likely. He passed away in 1842 in Calloway County at the age of seventy-nine.

There are markers for people who fought in just about every American War leading up to World War II. There are also tombstones with hand-etched lettering on them. Some very strange graves also lie within Asbury. Upon some of the concrete blocks that mark graves for those too poor to afford regular stones, there are gears. The purpose of the gears is unknown. We couldn't find an explanation for such a marker. However, there is something about Asbury even more interesting than the gear-marked blocks.

Scattered about the graveyard, you can find small metal pipes protruding from the ground. At first, most people might wonder about the purpose of these pipes. These pipes are there for those buried alive – a common mistake in the days before medical advancements in embalming and determining if someone was deceased. Some graveyards had bells placed near graves with strings tied to the corpses' fingers, so if the undertakers buried them alive, they could ring the bell when they awoke. In this case, these pipes were there so the person lying in the grave could breathe and call for help.

With so many veterans buried there, and with the possibility that some folks experienced living burial, it isn't shocking that Asbury Graveyard is haunted.

Asbury is sort of a Lover's Lane in Calloway County. Doubtless, it is due to its seclusion and the many trees surrounding it. Through the years, couples have parked there, or wandered into the cemetery, to be alone. Some of them, however, have come back with some chilling tales to tell.

In the 1960s, a couple parked at Asbury to be alone. Before long, they heard scratching against the back bumper. Thinking it was an animal or perhaps a small tree branch, they ignored it. After a few more minutes passed, the scratching grew louder and more intense. This time, they stopped to look. That's when they noticed no trees were near them. As they sat quietly a few more seconds, debating whether to check it out, go back to business, or just drive off, an oppressive sense of dread settled upon them. The car began to shake, as if something was bouncing on the bumper. This spurred the couple into action and they quickly drove out of there.

They never did find out what caused the car to shake, so they could only speculate. It's possible a heavy animal could have done it. It wouldn't have been a person because they would have been visible through the back window. Of course, it could have been a resident specter trying to get a better look.

Two couples who heard the graveyard was haunted parked near Asbury on a cold dark night. As they sat in the car, they heard a strange noise outside. At first, the noise was faint, as if far away but drawing closer. In a few seconds, they heard what they thought was the sound of horse hooves galloping across the ground. They looked hard into the darkness but never saw a horse. They found themselves startled by the loud and distinct sound of a horse snorting just outside the car. Still, they saw no horse.

This spooked them good, so the driver started the car and sped away. As the car raced down the road, they could still hear the sound of hooves, only pounding harder. Still, there was no horse. It didn't take long before the galloping reached the car. No matter how hard the driver pressed the accelerator, he could not shake whatever was making the noise. Again, they heard the loud snort. They drove on, hearing these sounds coming from what they presumed to be a ghost horse. After a few more miles, the sounds ended.

There are reports of eerie shadow people moving around the graves, and near the cemetery trees. These figures often bring with them a deep and nearly maddening sense of fear. Witnesses report feeling as though they are being watched, even in daylight, then the dread would settle upon them. Soon after, the shadows would move around the graveyard.

Another incident occurred as a young man was cutting through the cemetery on his way home from work. As he passed beneath the shadow of the hemlock trees, he looked up and saw someone coming his way. When the person drew nearer, he said, "How-do?" Right after the woman passed, he realized he knew her face. She was a woman who died just days before, and he had attended her funeral. Shocked by this revelation, the young man turned around to get another look – but she was gone. He then ran home, and upon entering his house he declared, "Never bury me at Asbury Cemetery. That place is haunted!"

JACOB FLOYD AND JENNY FLOYD

THE THIN MAN'S GRAVE

Kentucky's Haunted Mansions
Kentucky's Strange and Unusual Haunts

If you have read our book, *Kentucky's Haunted Mansions*, then you know the tale of the Sexton House in Russellville with the image of a female bather burned into the window by a lightning bolt. The sexton of the Sexton House is the groundskeeper of the Maple Grove Cemetery located on the property. Allegedly, the young lady immortalized by lightning haunts the Sexton House, and the graveyard is haunted as well.

Maple Grove is an expansive, opened cemetery with long-reaching rows of stones. There are a few rumors about the people buried within, as well as former residents of the Sexton House, haunting the grounds. Though, as with so many local legends, historical details are scarce.

Shadows stroll the cemetery both day and night. Unexplained orbs float through the darkness. One man visiting the grave of a family member at night saw a strange streak of bluish-white light a few yards from where he stood. The wisp moved erratically, so he went to check the source, wondering if someone needed help. As he approached, the light dimmed. When he came upon the spot where he believed he had seen it, no one was there, and the grounds were once again dark. He looked around and called to see if anyone was there, and then suddenly, a man spoke behind him, making him jump.

"Why are you here?" the voice spoke.

He turned to see a thin pale man with no hair, a few inches taller than he, standing just inches behind him. He told the man he was visiting someone's plot and the man said, "Go away. You're standing on my grave."

The man looked down and saw a tombstone behind him. He looked at it for a second to try to see the name and dates, but couldn't make them out because of the age. When he turned around to apologize, the man was gone.

Chilled by the experience, the man left Maple Grove without looking back. Though the incident seemed paranormal, he maintains it was probably someone who wasn't in their right mind hanging out in the graveyard, which was spooky enough for him, and is the reason he left. But, he does admit that the encounter was unsettling and the man rather unnerving. He'd heard stories when he was younger about a generic man in a black suit that supposedly walking the graveyard at night, but chalks it up to coincidence. He has never seen the man since going back.

However, that is not the only haunted Maple Grove Cemetery in Kentucky. The other is located on Taylorsville Road in the Nelson County town of Bloomfield, haunted by Ann Coke Beauchamp. In 1825, Anne's husband, Jereboam O. Beauchamp, murdered former Kentucky attorney general Col. Solomon Sharp over a rumor that Sharp had fathered an illegitimate son with Ann. This led to an enraged Jereboam going to Sharp's home and stabbing him to death.

Jereboam was to swing from the gallows on July 7th, 1826. The jailer permitted Ann to stay with her husband in his cell during his final days of life. On July 5th, the couple attempted suicide by taking laudanum. This attempt did not work. On the day Jereboam was to die, Ann convinced the guard to let them have a few minutes alone. Unbeknownst to the guard, Ann had managed to smuggle in a knife, and the both of them attempted suicide once again, this time by slitting their wrists.

When the guard returned, he found both Beauchamps bleeding out. Guards quickly carried Jereboam to the gallows and hanged him by the neck until he died. Ann died in the cell from her self-inflicted wounds. The two were buried in each other's arms at Maple Grove Cemetery.

For some reason, Ann seems cursed to wander the land around the graveyard. Witnesses hear her cries in the evening. Her pale apparition walks around her grave. Some say she also wanders the road in front of Maple Grove. She appears dejected, downtrodden, and eternally sad. Could this be because Jereboam has yet to forgive her for the unfaithfulness, and she remains unaccepted into the grave they share?

VICTOR'S LOUISVILLE

Haunts of Hollywood Stars and Starlets

JACOB FLOYD AND JENNY FLOYD

Born in Louisville, Ky. on January 29th, 1913, Victor Mature had a humble beginning. His mother was a Kentucky native of Swiss heritage and his father was a cutler from the small town of Pinzolo in the Italian Alps. He also had a brother who died at the age of eleven. Mature attended St. Xavier High School eventually took on odd jobs prior to leaving for Hollywood.

For three years, he lived in a tent and studied acting at the Pasadena Community Playhouse. During his time there, he appeared in more than sixty plays. Famed TV and film producer, Hal Roach, took notice of him and landed him a minor role in the 1939 film, *My Housekeeper's Daughter*. In 1940, he starred alongside Lon Cheney Jr. in *One Million B.C.*, which gained him notoriety as a well-built sex symbol. After that, Mature received many roles that utilized his handsome features. But, he didn't want to be the type of actor who could only get by on his looks. So, he began seeking out a variety of roles. He scored a hit in the musical play, *Lady in the Dark,* and had some minor success with smaller films that followed. Soon after, he became a commodity and different producers requested him for their films. Mature bought out his contract in full and found himself making $1500 a week with numerous film commitments lined up. Among the hits he strung together during the early 40s were *Seven Days' Leave*, *My Gal Sal*, *I Wake up Screaming*, and *Footlight Serenade*.

Mature halted his career in 1942 to enlist for service in World War II. The Navy rejected him due to his colorblindness, but the Coast Guard accepted him. He never saw battle and received an honorable discharge in 1945.

Upon returning to his film career, he turned in two of his most famous performances: John Ford's *My Darling Clementine* and the role of Doc Holliday in *Wyatt Earp*. Then, in contrast to those roles, he starred in the thriller *Moss Rose*, the noir *Kiss of Death*, and his first Western, *Fury at Furnace Creek*, all of which were hits that reinforced his stardom. His most famous role was as Samson in Cecil B. DeMille's epic *Samson and Delilah*. The film was a major success and was the frontrunner of the coming trend of big budget productions set in some period of the ancient world.

Mature then starred in the first Cinemascope film, *The Robe*, which was the first of two films where he would play the role of Demetrius—the other being the 1954 sequel, *Demetrius and the Gladiators*. Over the next few years, he signed numerous deals with different companies and starred in many more films. In 1958, he made his first film for his own production company, Romina Productions, called *China Doll*. A few more films followed before Mature decided to retire at the age of 46.

Despite retirement, Mature did a few more films in his life, mainly comedic roles, a couple of which poked fun at his own acting style. Mature made several jokes about himself and his acting abilities through the years, and even admitted that he was more interested in making money than acting, stating that he only wanted to make enough money to retire at a decent age and enjoy living life as a loafer.

Despite being married five times, Victor only had one child: a daughter named Victoria, who he had with his last wife, Loretta G. Sebena (1974-99). His other wives were Frances Charles (1938-40), Martha Stephenson Kemp

(1941-43), Dorothy Standford Berry (1948-55), and Adrian Joy Urwick (1959-69).

Mature died of leukemia at his home in Rancho Santa Fe, California in 1999 at the age of 86. His body lies at the Mature Family plot in St. Michael's Cemetery in his hometown of Louisville, Kentucky. His fans still come to pay their respects to him by placing various tokens on his grave.

Despite being a major star, Mature received a lot of criticism for his acting. There were those that appreciated his style, but it wasn't until many years later that critics began to respect his work; some have even claimed that he was quite underrated. Though he may have had his detractors, none can deny his success. His work entertained moviegoers for many years. In the end, that's what being in the movie business is all about.

Though there have not been any major or extensive accounts of spectral encounters at his gravesite, there have been some EVPs captured by other ghost hunters. One was a quote from one of Mature's films, and the other was a very angry response that sounded like someone cussing at the investigators, though nothing here actually indicates the latter was Victor Mature.

When Jenny and I heard of these alleged EVPs, we decided to seek out his grave. While there, we managed to get a few responses on the spirit box. We heard the name "Victor" twice. Other than that, we didn't experience anything other than a welcoming vibe around the plot.

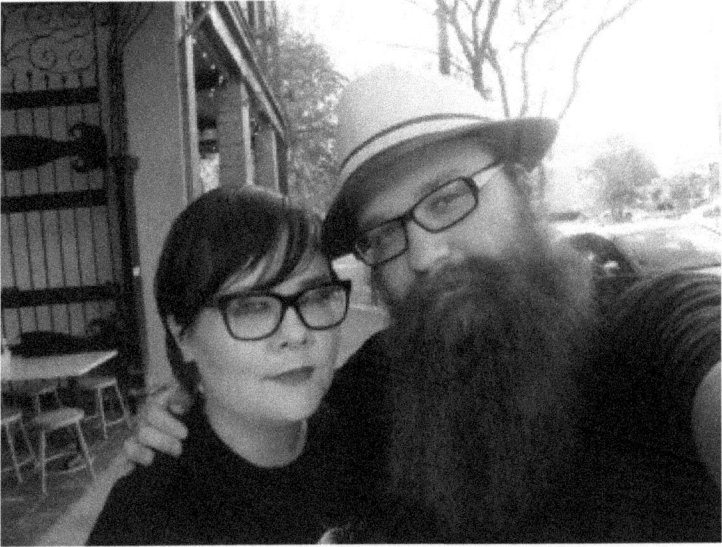

Jenny and Jacob Floyd, known as the Frightening Floyds, live in Shepherdsville with their cats and rabbits. They enjoy ghosts, aliens, cryptids, Disney, horror, and a bunch of strange and unusual things.

ALSO AVAILABLE FROM NIGHTMARE PRESS

OCCULTATION

Eric Lahti

On a long-abandoned alien space station orbiting a mysterious black object, the rules are different. Whether it's the immersive virtual reality that's indistinguishable from reality, the wild bazaar where anything and everything is for sale, the drunken debauchery, or the group of giants who run everything and keep the peace, Endpoint is the place where people go to do what they'd never do anywhere else.

For instance, two nights ago a hacker deleted her brain. This morning a thief awoke in her body with a task: *Find out what happened and you'll get your body back.*

Now, Nat will have to navigate the madness, cults, and twisted power structures to find answers. But on Endpoint, nothing is ever simple.

And the abandoned alien space station may not be as abandoned as everyone thought.

ALADDIN'S CURSE

Mark Pickvet

A magic lamp containing an evil Djinni embarks upon an incredible journey as it passes from the Stone Age to the Modern World. The malevolent Djinni fulfills the wishes of those who gain possession of his lamp, only those wishes do not always come out exactly as planned. Tragedy fills *Aladdin's Curse,* as little to no good comes to those who wish for personal gain from the ancient magic. Only three unselfish wishes can rid the world of this wicked force. Follow the series of subplots and short stories through time as the lamp and the evil spirit within all uniquely interconnect them.

The dark side of human nature is only a wish away. As the old saying goes: "Be careful what you wish for; you just might get it!"

BREAKING THE DEVIL'S BREAD:

DARK WORDS AND SHADOW TALES

Satyros Phil Brucato

Our lives are made of stories.

Some of those tales get pretty damn dark.

In the following "13 stories and an Oops," award-winning dark fantasist Satyros Phil Brucato (*Red Shoes, Mage, Valhalla with a Twist of Lethe*) explores shadows, cries, and silence.

Careless haunters, elite collectors, secretive enforcers, lip-synching goths, hapless custodians, strange children, subterranean exiles, tortured fiends, harried jesters, haggard coulrophobes, ragged batterers, joyous hikers, carnal mystics, and exploding cosmos tell their tales as sardonic darkness swallows all.

If mortal dread is the Devil's bread, then we're all welcome at the feast.

THE HURDY GURDY MAN

David Turnbull

Set in London in the summer of 1969, *The Hurdy Gurdy Man* follows Kath Dunn, who has left her home near the seaside town Berwick on Tweed, and finds herself homeless on the streets of Piccadilly. Here she encounters the eccentric Gordon Urquhart-Scott, who persuades Kath to accompany him to his large crumbling home on the edge of Hampstead Heath, where he claims to run a hostel for homeless women.

Kath finds herself inducted as one of twelve formerly homeless women who reside free of charge in the house in exchange for obeying the Hurdy Gurdy Man's strange rules, including nightly musical performances on the hand-cranked hurdy-gurdy from which his nickname derives.

Kath befriends Ruth. Together they secretly unravel terrible truths linked to the British Class system, the establishment, and the gruesome Scottish borders legends of the Redcaps. After witnessing how deep the horror within the decaying home truly runs, the two women decide to confront the evil at its source. Enlisting the help of other women, they engineer a terrifying conflict they hope will send the evil back to whatever foul region of darkness from whence it came.

BELINDA'S KEYBOARDS
PART ONE: DED'S LINE

Dedham Pond

Dedham Pond is a journalist in his fifties rediscovering how to do his job responsibly in an era that appreciates bias over truth and influencers over experts. While investigating the death of an old friend's son, Ded discovers Belinda Blessing, who is part of a conspiracy of people who enjoy injecting discord and chaos into the culture wherever they can. Now Ded must find a way to stop the destruction caused by Belinda's keyboards and bring her to justice.

SARAH CORBIN'S BLOODY REVENGE

Coyote Wallace

When Sarah Corbin and her family are killed in a midnight robbery gone wrong, she makes a deal for her mortal soul - in exchange for the chance to hunt down the men who burned her world to ash.

Violent, unflinching, and tinged with supernatural overtones, *Sarah Corbin's Bloody Revenge* takes readers into the dark heart of Texas, where the air is heavy with gun smoke and the streets run red.

On the other end of Sarah's revenge is Lono Talbot, a murderous cutthroat who has parlayed stolen gold into a position of power in the small town of Gehenna. His network of gunslingers and outlaws, reinforced with his ill-gotten gains, has made him one of the most powerful men in the Texas underground. Too well protected for lawmen, Lono continues to grow his influence and power....

....until the mistakes of his past come calling.

MURKY SHADOWS

Belinda Brady

Welcome to *Murky Shadows*, a deliciously dark world where ghosts, ghouls, monsters and all-too-horrifying realities collide, and vampires, ghosts and things that go bump in the night rule. From a vengeful fairy, to a bloodthirsty roommate, to the ghosts of a serial killer plotting their revenge, no supernatural stone is left unturned in this captivating collection of spooky tales.

Murky Shadows, by Belinda Brady, is a treasure of short stories that will take you to places you never dreamed possible, and introduce you to characters you would only meet in your worst nightmares. So sit back, relax, perhaps put a light on, and delve into this chilling mixed bag of dark stories, one that not only brings the supernatural to life, but also taps into the darkest corners of the human psyche.

Which story will be your favorite?

NO ONE CAN SAVE US

Kendall Phillips

Adam always keeps his powers in check. As the world's only superhero, he must know his limits. Defeat the master criminal, repel an army, stop a natural disaster, but never let himself go too far.

Until Syangnom.

The world has grown accustomed to the feats of its only superhuman. Adam's wife, Sara, a celebrated journalist and periodic hostage, regularly reports his exploits, and the agents of Extra-Judicial Affairs handle all the legal issues.

But when Adam becomes enraged in the reclusive regime of Syangnom, he leaves 14 million people dead and the world recoiling from the destruction he has wrought.

Now Adam's wife Sara and EJA Agent Kia Mercado must track down the conspiracy behind Adam's breakdown and discover the otherworldly source of his powers. Their search will bring them face to face with supervillains, eldritch gods, and the mysterious figure who defends Chicago from the shadows, the armored hero known only as No One.

A SOUL A DAY

Todd Sullivan

What lengths would you go to save a soul?

In the shadows of South Korea, Min Jae rebels against the Gwanlyo, an organization of vampires that tempts mortals with power, money, sex, and the promise of immortality. The catch? An eternity in Hell.

Min Jae will stop at nothing to prevent another human from becoming a vampire. He embarks on a holy quest to save those marked for damnation. Next on his list— Desmond, an expat in Seoul who lives an ordinary life of work and friends.

To stave off the Gwanlyo hellbent on acquiring Desmond, Min Jae enlists the services of Hyeri, a serial killer turned vampire who hates the organization for her own insane reasons. Will the unlikely pair be able to rescue Desmond before he becomes a vampire? Will the undead organization keep the duo from disrupting their plans?

Find out in A SOUL A DAY, a tale of violence, madness, and redemption.

SCROLLS OF RAMOSE, SCRIBE OF EGYPT

James Arthur Anderson

According to the Book of Exodus, God cast ten deadly plagues against Egypt and the Pharaoh for his enslavement of the Israelites. One wonders what it must have been like to be an ordinary Egyptian, innocent of Ramesses II's transgressions, yet still suffering the wrath of the Almighty.

Scrolls of Ramose, Scribe of Egypt retells the story from the point of view of the chief scribe of Ramesses the Great, and relives the suffering the people of the Two Lands endured during the plagues of the bloody Nile: the infestations of frogs, insects, and boils; the terror of fiery hail and darkness; and finally, the death of the eldest sons.

You have heard the stories, now see them through the eyes of the innocent merely trying to survive the deadly hand of an angry God.

STITCHES AND OTHER STORIES

J.M. Heluk

Nothing in *Stitches and Other Stories* is what it seems, leaving the reader to speculate on the origin of its horror—to root out those subtle connections and, ultimately, stitch each tale together on their own.

Stitches and Other Stories was designed to make the reader an active participant. In the end, you decide the genesis of the horror.

From a family stranded by an unnatural force on their Montana farm in "Two Miles as the Crow Flies," to "Stitches," the story of a young boy terrorized by his dead grandmother. Meet a temperamental little girl from a New York City slum who possesses a deadly talent in "The Wishman and the Worm." In "The Ovid," something has come home to roost in a less-than-quaint seaside town.

Sit back and let *Stitches and Other Stories* guide you through a frightful landscape while you read deep into the night.

JENNY'S SPOOKY LITTLE TALES: VOL. 2

The Frightening Floyds have been researching and writing about the paranormal and all things strange and unusual for ten years. To celebrate, Jenny recently compiled ten of her favorite stories from the many books she has written with her husband Jacob, which became *Jenny's Spooky Little Tales: Vol. 1*. Now, she has compiled ten more for *Jenny's Spooky Little Tales: Vol. 2*.

In this collection, you'll find ghosts, a meat shower, a haunted Disney World attraction, spirits of Hollywood stars and starlets, the Bermuda Triangle, and even spooky tales from Louisville's famed Churchill Downs. We hope you enjoy *Jenny's Spooky Little Tales: Vol. 2*.

READ MORE NIGHTMARE PRESS!!!

Visit our website at nightmarepress5.wordpress.com

Also, follow us on:

Facebook: https://www.facebook.com/nightmarepress1

Instagram: https://www.instagram.com/nightmarepress1

Join the Nightmare Press Group on Facebook to interact with our authors, and to keep abreast of their creative endeavors.